Slang Rules!

A PRACTICAL GUIDE FOR ENGLISH LEARNERS

Orin Hargraves

Illustrated by Anthony Jenkins

Merriam-Webster, Incorporated
Springfield, Massachusetts, U.S.A.

A GENUINE MERRIAM-WEBSTER

The name *Webster* alone is no guarantee of excellence. It is used by a number of publishers and may serve mainly to mislead an unwary buyer.

Merriam-Webster™ is the name you should look for when you consider the purchase of dictionaries or other fine reference books. It carries the reputation of a company that has been publishing since 1831 and is your assurance of quality and authority.

Copyright © 2008 by Orin Hargraves

ISBN: 978-087779-682-4

Library of Congress Cataloging-in-Publication Data

Hargraves, Orin.
  Slang rules! : a practical guide for English learners / Orin Hargraves.
      p. cm.
  Includes index.
  ISBN 978-0-87779-682-4
  1. English language—Slang—Dictionaries.
  2. English language—Textbooks for foreign speakers. I. Title.
  PE2846.H36 2008
  427'.09—dc22

                                                              2008033245

Excerpt from *Jackie Brown: A Screenplay*, by Quentin Tarantino. Copyright © 1997 by Quentin Tarantino. Used by permission of Hyperion Books. All rights reserved.

Made in the United States of America

54321QW/V1211100908

This book is dedicated to the many friends

who, over the years, have invited me

to cross the cultural divide

on the bridge of English;

particularly to

Maati, Majid, Irfan, and Nobo

Acknowledgments

I would like to thank Hyperion Books for permission to excerpt the Quentin Tarantino screenplay, and Desert Storm Records for the lyric by Fabolous. Several bloggers were kind enough to let me quote extensively from their excellent blogs, providing good and genuine material for illustrating the use of slang; I would especially like to thank Chevonne Collins, Ted Johnson, and Tracy X.

The book would have been all but unimaginable without the lively, apt, and vivid drawings of Anthony Jenkins. Loree Hany laid out the pages with style and sensitivity. Finally, I am especially grateful to my editor and friend at Merriam-Webster, Mark Stevens, whose patient care and detailed attention have contributed immeasurably to the merits of this book.

Orin Hargraves
Westminster, MD

Contents

Pronunciation Symbols

Consonants

b	**b**a**b**y, la**b**or, ca**b**
d	**d**ay, ki**d**, ri**dd**le
dʒ	**j**ust, ba**dg**er, fu**dge**
ð	**th**en, ei**th**er, ba**th**e
f	**f**oe, tou**gh**, bu**ff**
g	**g**o, da**gg**er, ba**g**
h	**h**ot, a**h**ead
j	**y**es, vine**y**ard
k	**c**at, flo**ck**, s**k**in
l	**l**aw, ho**ll**ow
ļ	peda**l**, batt**l**e, fina**l**
m	**m**at, he**m**p, ha**mm**er
n	**n**ew, te**n**t, te**n**or, ru**n**
ņ	butto**n**, sati**n**, kitte**n**
ŋ	ru**ng**, ha**ng**, swi**ng**er
p	to**p**, s**p**eed, **p**ay
r	**r**ope, a**rr**ive
s	**s**ad, mi**s**t, ki**ss**
ʃ	**sh**oe, mi**ss**ion, slu**sh**
t	s**t**ick, la**t**e, la**t**er
tʃ	ba**tch**, na**t**ure, **ch**oose
θ	**th**in, e**th**er, ba**th**
v	**v**at, ne**v**er, ca**v**e
w	**w**et, soft**w**are
z	**z**oo, ea**s**y, bu**zz**
ʒ	vi**s**ion, a**z**ure, bei**ge**

Vowels

æ	**a**sk, b**a**t, gl**a**d
ɑː	c**o**t, b**o**mb, p**a**w
ɛ	b**e**t, f**e**d
ə	**a**bout, ban**a**na, collide
iː	**ea**t, b**ea**d, b**ee**
ɪ	**i**d, b**i**d, p**i**t
ʊ	f**oo**t, sh**ou**ld, p**u**t
uː	b**oo**t, tw**o**, c**oo**
ʌ	**u**nder, p**u**tt, b**u**d
ɚ	m**er**ge, b**ir**d, furth**er**
eɪ/ej	**eigh**t, w**a**de, pl**a**y
aɪ/aj	**i**ce, b**i**te, t**i**le
aʊ/aw	**ou**t, g**ow**n, **ow**l
ɔɪ/oj	**oy**ster, c**oi**l, b**oy**
oʊ/ow	**oa**t, **ow**n, z**o**ne
ɑɚ/ɑr	c**ar**, h**ear**t, st**ar**
eɚ/er	b**are**, f**air**, w**ear**
iɚ/ir	n**ear**, d**eer**, m**ere**
oɚ/or	b**oar**, p**or**t, d**oor**
uɚ/ur	b**oor**, t**our**

Other Symbols

ˈ	high stress: **pen**manship
ˌ	low stress: penman**ship**
/	slash used in pairs to mark the beginning and end of a pronunciation or set of pronunciations /ˈpɛn/

SLANG FAQ

What is slang?

Slang is the language that people often use in speaking and writing informally.

Who uses slang?

Everyone. Anyone whose first language is English uses English slang at some time.

When do people use slang?

People use slang when talking with their friends and family members. They may also use it when they first meet someone of their own age. Especially for young people, conversing in slang is a way to find out what things they have in common.

Is slang difficult to learn?

No. In most ways, slang is easier than the English you learn in the classroom. But you will need practice in order to understand when you're hearing slang.

Is slang difficult to speak?

No. Slang is easier to speak than standard English because most of the words are simpler and some rules of grammar are not as important.

Can I use slang anytime?

No. People usually do *not* use slang in these situations:
- when speaking to people in official positions, such as teachers or police officers
- when speaking on the telephone with someone they don't know well
- when speaking formally—for example, in a meeting at work
- when speaking with strangers

Is slang offensive?

Most slang isn't offensive. But using slang in formal-language situations isn't appropriate, and someone might take offense if you do.

Does slang include some offensive words?

Yes. All the slang words in this book that may be offensive are marked, and you should never use them around people who might be offended by them. Some words are offensive mostly to particular groups; these words are also identified in this book.

How do I know if a word is slang?

It's not always easy! Many words have double lives, with both slang and standard meanings. Most English-learners only know that a word is slang when they ask a native English-speaker—and even native speakers may disagree! This book should give you a good understanding of how Americans use slang, so that you'll be able to speak to anyone with confidence!

How do I learn slang?

By studying this book! It will help you to understand the three main aspects of slang:

Words

The easiest part of learning slang is learning new words. Although there are many slang words, they are not difficult to learn. They are often shorter and more fun than other words, and most of them are related to words that you already know.

Pronunciation

When people talk informally, they usually don't pronounce their words carefully, and some sounds get left out or changed. Also, some words may have a special pronunciation that is different from the one you learned in school. This book will show you the common ways that American slang is pronounced. It will also show you how ordinary words may be spelled when they are being used as slang.

Grammar

In informal English, some rules of grammar are ignored. However, you can't simply choose which rules you will ignore—there is a clear difference between speaking informally and speaking incorrectly! This book will show you which rules of grammar change, and which rules are sometimes ignored, when speaking slang.

ABOUT THE UNITS

There are 66 units in this book: 4 in the introduction, 53 in the main section, and 9 in the final section. Most of them follow the same plan: new language is introduced and illustrated, and then a set of exercises gives you a chance to use the new language you have learned. Five of the units (Units 17, 20, 50, 51, and 59) have no exercises, but they are just as important as the others!

The new vocabulary in this book is almost always introduced in a standard way, like this:

> **pass out** *phrasal verb* faint; lose consciousness (sometimes as a result of drugs or alcohol)

The term in boldface (like **this**) is the vocabulary item. It may include the symbol ⇌ ; see Unit 10 for an explanation. Following a boldface term, you may find a pronunciation written in the International Phonetic Alphabet (IPA), but only for words that you might get wrong. (Most slang is easy to pronounce. When an ordinary word is used as slang, it may have a "slang spelling" that shows its pronunciation even more clearly. We'll look at this subject later.)

The term in italics (like *this*) is a function label. The following function labels are used: *noun, verb, phrasal verb, abbreviation, adverb, adjective, predicate adjective.* (A *predicate adjective* is an adjective that is used after a verb but not before a noun.) In the definitions of phrasal verbs and idioms, **sb** stands for "somebody," and **sth** stands for "something."

Following the function label, you will find a definition or explanation of the word or idiom.

Only the *slang* vocabulary is treated this way. Most of the standard English words that are used in the book will be familiar to you; those that you don't know can be found in any dictionary.

About Offensive Language

Some slang is offensive, and all offensive slang in this book is labeled. If you wish to learn slang thoroughly, you must learn what the offensive words mean. But you don't have to use them! Even when you're communicating with your close friends, always think carefully about whether an offensive word is a good choice. Those who avoid offensive language altogether can enjoy the respect of everyone, since bad language almost always makes a bad impression on people. Beware!

Doing the Exercises

All the exercises in this book can be done in written and spoken form. It is important to do *both!* Writing will help you remember what you have learned; speaking will give you practice at pronouncing slang and using it naturally. If possible, work on the exercises together with a friend—you'll both learn more and have fun doing it!

Getting the Hang of Slang

When you get the hang of something, you understand it well enough to use it or do it yourself. Getting the hang of American slang requires three things:
1. Recognizing and learning new words
2. Understanding informal and shortened pronunciation
3. Understanding when grammar is simplified in slang expressions

In the four units that follow, you'll learn some slang greetings. By learning them, you'll also learn how the rest of the book will go about teaching you American slang.

Yo!

There are many different ways to say "Hello" in English. The second part of most greetings, in which you ask the person how he or she is, also may take many different forms.

Friends use slang greetings when they meet each other. See how this group of friends says hello:

What does it all mean?

Words that mean "Hello": **Hi**, **Hiya** /ˈhajə/, **Hey**, **Howdy**, and **Yo** are all different ways to greet someone. All these words are more informal than *Hello*. Sometimes **Hey** and **Yo** are also used simply to get someone's attention.

What you call people when you don't use their names: In this book you'll learn many slang words that friends use to address each other. Here are the ones used in the drawing above:

dude: a man (but sometimes people say **dude** when addressing a female)

guys: (plural) a group of people, male or female

peeps: (plural, short for "people") your good friends

What you say next: After people say "Hello," they nearly always ask something like "How are you?" or "What's happening?" In the conversation above, there are two expressions that mean "What's happening?": **'Sup?** and **Que pasa?** /keɪˈpɑːsɑ/ .

Look at some of the other ways that people ask "How are you?" as the conversation continues:

Here are some questions that people use to make a friendly inquiry:

How's it goin'?

Whatcha been up to?
(= What have you been up to?)

What's shakin'?

What's new with you?

How ya doin'?
(= How are you doing?)

The unusual spellings in these questions (and also in **'Sup?**) show how they are pronounced. We'll look at ways that slang changes spelling and pronunciation in later units.

Try It!

One person's speech is missing in each of the four groups below. Write a suitable greeting, question, or response in each of the blank speech balloons.

1.
Hey. How's it goin'?

2.
Suzanne! Whatcha been up to?

3.
Howdy Ray

4.
Not a thing. How 'bout you?

Gimme a Break!

When people use slang, they may pronounce ordinary words differently from the way they're pronounced in formal or standard English. A word can sound very different depending on the way it's pronounced.

☹ **The bad news:** Slang pronunciation is sometimes almost unrelated to the way that a word is normally spelled.

☺ **The good news:** Slang pronunciation is often much easier than standard English pronunciation.

When writing slang and informal English, it's usual to spell words differently. This "slang spelling" shows the reader that slang is being used and shows more clearly how it is pronounced, since slang spelling is always based on the way that words are actually spoken. Here are some examples that you have already seen:

You is often pronounced /jə/ in informal speech. The spelling *ya* shows this more accurately.

Many Americans drop the final *-g* when they pronounce verbs that end in *–ing*. Writers usually put an apostrophe (') after the last *n* to show this, but not always. (Be careful: The final *–g* is mostly dropped from verbs!)

Contractions—*what's* (= what is, what has), *you've* (= you have), *they're* (= they are), etc.—normally include an apostrophe to show where letters have been left out. But in slang, contractions are often spelled without the apostrophe.

Slang uses many more contractions than standard English. The pronunciation of slang contractions is often very different from their standard pronunciation. Sometimes writers use different spelling to show how the words are pronounced:

"**'Sup?**" /'sʌp/ (= What's up?)

"**Whatcha** been up to?" /'wʌtʃə/ (= What have you)

"I'm **sposta** meet Drew and Rachel here." /'spoʊstə/ (= supposed to)

WHATCHA

How do you get **whatcha** from "what have you"?

1. Get rid of *have*. This leaves "what you."

2. Since *you* is often pronounced /jə/ and spelled *ya*, this leaves "what ya."

3. When a /t/ sound is followed by a /j/ sound, as in "what ya," this sound becomes /tʃ/. To show this pronunciation, people often use the spelling **whatcha**. Later we'll see other similar words like **gotcha** and **betcha**.

Recognizing and using informal contractions is a very important part of learning slang. We'll look at many of the ways that slang combines words in future units.

Try It!

Here are some sentences written using "slang spelling." See if you can rewrite them in standard English:

1. What's shakin'? _____

2. How're ya gettin' home? _____

3. Where'd ya go last night? _____

4. Why's it takin' so long? _____

5. Why's it taken so long? _____

Say What?

When people use slang, some rules of grammar are ignored or relaxed.

☹ **The bad news:** You can't choose which rules of grammar to ignore when you speak slang. There's a clear difference between speaking slang and speaking incorrectly!

☺ **The good news:** With slang, you don't always have to follow some of the more difficult rules of English grammar.

Here are some ways we've seen grammar change when people speak slang.

Short verb forms, especially in questions, are often dropped (that is, not pronounced) in slang speech:

"Where ya headed?" = Where are you headed?
"How ya doin'?" = How are you doing?

The verbs that are most often dropped in slang are *will* and forms of *be*. Sometimes a form of *have* (either *have* or *has*) or a form of *do* (*do, does,* or *did*) is also dropped. We'll look at cases where this happens in future units.

Idioms

You've probably learned many English idioms already. Many more are only used in slang and informal speech.

An idiom is a group of words with a particular meaning that is different from the combined meanings of all the individual words. In many slang idioms, the grammar may also be unusual.

Long time no see! means "I haven't seen you in a long time." People say this when they're happy—and perhaps surprised—to see you again after a long time.

What's with the _____? When you want someone to explain something, you can ask "What's with the _____?" This question is very informal, an expression that friends use with each other, but not one that you would use with someone to whom you normally show respect.

The title of this unit is also an idiom, one that's used mostly by black Americans. **Say what?** is a way of asking "What did you say?" It wouldn't be polite to use it with someone you don't know, but friends use it with each other all the time.

The title of Unit B is also an idiom. **Gimme a break!** (= Give me a break!) usually means "That's ridiculous!" or "Stop criticizing me!" Again, it's fine to use it with your friends, but not with people who you don't know.

Try It!

Write the standard English equivalent of each of these slang questions. Look for contractions, slang spellings, and verbs that have been left out.

EXAMPLE: Where ya goin'? _____ *Where are you going?* _____

1. Anybody sittin' here? _____

2. Whatcha got in the box? _____

3. How long ya been waitin' here? _____

4. You know that guy over there? _____

5. Why she drivin' your car? _____

Word!

The easiest part of learning slang is learning new words.

☹ **The bad news:** Sometimes it's difficult to find room in your head for lots of new vocabulary!

☺ **The good news:** Most slang words and expressions are related to words that you already know.

The Way to Remember

The best way to remember a new slang word is by mentally linking it with another word or phrase that you already know.

Many slang words are either (1) short forms of one or more other words, or (2) standard words with a slightly different meaning.

Words that are formed by shortening

We have already seen some words that are a shortened form of one or more other words:

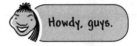

Howdy, guys.

Howdy: You know the polite greeting "How do you do?" An older form of this phrase was "How do ye?" If you say this quickly, it sounds like **Howdy**—an informal way of saying "Hello."

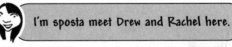

I'm sposta meet Drew and Rachel here.

sposta: This is a slang spelling of "supposed to," which is pronounced /ˈspoʊstə/ in informal speech.

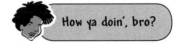

How ya doin', bro?

bro: In *bro* /ˈbroʊ/, part of a word has been thrown away. The longer word is one you already know: *brother*. (This is a common way of creating new slang words, which experts call *clipping*.)

Words that have another standard meaning

Many common words have a different meaning when used as slang. The slang meaning is usually related to the standard meaning, often in a humorous way.

head: You already know the noun *head*, and you may have heard *head* used as a verb as well. To head somewhere is to move in that direction (since you usually turn your head in the direction that you're traveling). So "Where ya headed?" means "Where are you going?"

Que pasa?: Sometimes words are borrowed from another language to become slang in English. **Que pasa?** is an example of this; it means "What's happening?" in both Spanish and English. (But the Spanish *Qué* is usually written as simply *Que* in English.)

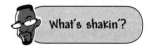

What's shakin'?: You already know the verb *shake*. If a thing is shaking, you can be sure that something is happening to it. So "What's shakin'?" simply means "What's happening?"

When you hear a new slang term that you don't understand, you should do two things: (1) Ask someone what it means (if possible), and (2) Mentally link the word with a word you already know.

Try It!

I. Look at the underlined slang words in the sentences below. Can you figure out what they mean? If not, look them up in the index. (You'll learn all these words in later units.) When you figure out what they mean, think of a way to remember them.

1. I know <u>zip</u> about calculus.

2. I must be going <u>bananas</u>.

3. He just signed a <u>mega</u> contract with a security firm.

4. I heard you <u>totaled</u> your car.

5. She got all defensive and <u>huffy</u> when I asked her.

6. Her brother's a <u>pothead</u> but he manages to hold down a job.

II. Column A below lists some slang words that you'll learn in future units. See if you can match them with the words they come from (in column B).

A	B
1. shoulda _____	A. parents
2. lemme _____	B. let me
3. ginormous _____	C. abdominals
4. abs _____	D. should have
5. 'rents _____	E. buddy
6. bud _____	F. gigantic + enormous

Slang Rules!

Get ready! This is where it starts getting fun.

The next 62 units form the main part of this book.

In each unit, you will do at least one of these three things:

1. Learn some new slang words and idioms.

2. Learn how slang is pronounced and spelled.

3. Learn which rules of grammar change slightly when people speak and write slang.

Some units focus on only one of these three things; some talk about all three.

Like the units you have already seen, the following units have exercises at the end. It's important to do the exercises *orally*—that is, to say them out loud. This will help you to remember what you've learned. But it's also important to *write* the exercises, so as to strengthen your new knowledge.

If you can, work on these units together with a friend. You both will learn more quickly, and you'll have fun doing it.

Who You Talkin' to?

You have seen some slang expressions—especially questions—that leave out auxiliary verbs (*have, does, is, are,* etc.); for example, **How ya doin'?** (= How are you doing?)

Here are some other questions that often leave out auxiliary verbs:

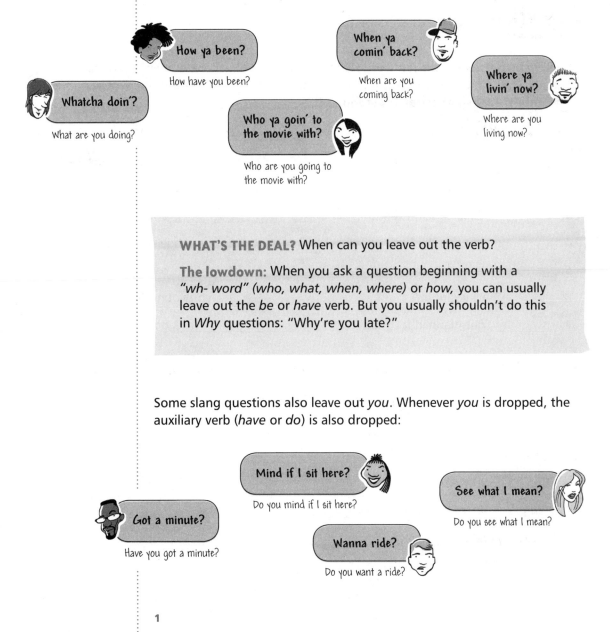

How ya been?

How have you been?

When ya comin' back?

When are you coming back?

Where ya livin' now?

Where are you living now?

Whatcha doin'?

What are you doing?

Who ya goin' to the movie with?

Who are you going to the movie with?

WHAT'S THE DEAL? When can you leave out the verb?

The lowdown: When you ask a question beginning with a *"wh- word"* (who, what, when, where) or *how*, you can usually leave out the *be* or *have* verb. But you usually shouldn't do this in *Why* questions: "Why're you late?"

Some slang questions also leave out *you*. Whenever *you* is dropped, the auxiliary verb (*have* or *do*) is also dropped:

Mind if I sit here?

Do you mind if I sit here?

See what I mean?

Do you see what I mean?

Got a minute?

Have you got a minute?

Wanna ride?

Do you want a ride?

WANNA?

Wanna /ˈwɑːnə/ may be a slang spelling of either "want a" or "want to":

"Wanna piece of chocolate?" (= Do you want a piece of chocolate?)
"Wanna go to the store?" (= Do you want to go to the store?)

Note that all the questions above are yes/no questions—questions that can be answered with "Yes" or "No"—and in standard English they begin with a helping verb.

Try It!

I. Fill in the missing question word (*who, whatcha, when, where,* **or** *how* **) in the following sentences. First read each sentence out loud! Then supply the missing words in the standard English question that follows it.**

EXAMPLE: *Where* ya sittin?   *Where* *are* you sitting?

1. _____ ya doin' with the new job?   _____ _____ you doing with the new job?

2. _____ ya rootin' for in the game?   _____ _____ you rooting for in the game?

3. _____ doin' this weekend?   _____ _____ _____ doing this weekend?

4. _____ ya been the last two hours?   _____ _____ you been the last two hours?

5. _____ ya comin' back from Dallas?   _____ _____ _____ coming back from Dallas?

6. _____ ya votin' for?   _____ _____ you voting for?

7. _____ got planned for Friday?   _____ _____ _____ got planned for Friday?

II. Read each of the following questions out loud. Then write the standard English version.

EXAMPLE: See where that oak tree is?   *Do you see where that oak tree is?*

1. Need a lift? _____

2. Got any ideas? _____

3. Mind if I borrow your watch? _____

4. Wanna see what I bought? _____

5. Seen any good movies lately? _____

6. Finished with that? _____

2

2 Chow Time

Let's put on the feedbag!

Many slang expressions are about eating:

chow *noun* food

chowhound *noun* a person who likes to eat a lot

grub *noun* food

down *verb* eat something

chow down *phrasal verb* eat, or start eating

pig out *phrasal verb* eat too much, or eat junk food

mack out *phrasal verb* eat too much

scarf up sth *phrasal verb* eat a lot of food quickly

dig in *phrasal verb* start eating

wolf sth ⇄ down *phrasal verb* eat something quickly

put on the feedbag *idiom* eat

shovel it in *idiom* eat a lot of food quickly

feed your face *idiom* eat

DID YOU KNOW?

Hound is another word for "dog." It's part of the name of some breeds of dog, like *bloodhound*, *foxhound*, and *wolfhound*.

Several slang words use *hound* to describe a person who likes something enough to hunt for it, like **chowhound** (a person who likes food). Other slang words with *-hound* are **boozehound**, **newshound**, and **rock hound.** See if you can guess what they mean!

What else is there to eat?

You know the ordinary meaning of *eat*, but it has slang meanings too. If you have to pay for something unfairly or against your wishes, then you "eat" the expense: "My son left the hotel without paying his bill and we had to eat it."

Eat is also used in different ways to talk about having oral sex. All of these terms are offensive or impolite. Two slang insults that friends often use with each other in a joking way are **Eat me!** and **Eat my shorts!**

Try It!

I. Use the words in the list that follows to fill in the blanks in the story.

| *pig out* | *down* | *chowhound* | *grub* | *wolf down* | *shovel it in* |

I don't think I'm that much of a _____, but after I finish working out I can really _____. My favorite thing to _____ on is macaroni and cheese: it's not the most healthy _____, but it cooks fast. I can usually _____ a whole box of it. My mom tells me I shouldn't _____ my food, but when you're hungry and in a hurry, that's what you gotta do!

II. Make your own sentences, filling in the blanks with the names of foods that you like. Be sure to read your sentences out loud!

1. Oh boy, _____! Can I dig in now?

2. I'm a real chowhound when it comes to _____.

3. I'm sorry to scarf up this _____ but I'm already late.

4. Let's get some chow! Are you hungry for _____?

3 Hot or Cool?

People often respond to new information by saying only one or two words. What do these words mean?

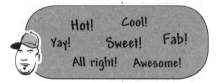

Hot! Cool!
Yay! Sweet! Fab!
All right! Awesome!

All these words mean almost the same thing. People say them when they like what someone has said or something that has happened.

People may use these expressions when they're happy and surprised by what they learn, hear, or see.

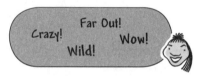

Crazy! Far Out! Wow!
Wild!

Gosh!
Wow!

People use these words when they hear surprising news that doesn't make them happy. Notice that people may say **"Wow!"** when they hear either positive or negative news.

Some other one-word responses have particular meanings:

You can say **"Bingo!"** when someone has figured out exactly what is happening or has suddenly realized the truth.

John didn't even speak to me at the party. Is he still mad about the game last week?

Bingo!

When someone tells you some bad news, you can say **"Bummer!"**

There's an accident on the bridge and the traffic is backed up for five miles.

Bummer!

People say **"Duh!"** when they think the answer to a question is very obvious.

Do you think I'll get a ticket if I park here?

Duh!

People say **"Uh-oh!"** /ˈʌˌoʊ/ when something bad has just happened, especially if it's something that can't be undone.

> All I did was turn this knob and then the trouble light came on and the alarm started.
>
> Uh-oh!

People sometimes say **"Whatever!"** in response to something that doesn't interest them, or as a way of expressing impatience.

> Do you think these pink ones are enough, or should I get some of the red ones and white ones too? Or maybe some of those orange ones?
>
> Whatever!

Some people say **"Word!"** or **"Word up!"** to show that they agree strongly with what someone else has said.

> This party sucks. Let's blow.
>
> Word up! I'm with ya, bro!"

Try It!

I. Read the sentences below and choose the word on the right that you think is the best response. Say the word out loud, then underline it.

EXAMPLE: They're giving away free CDs at the ticket booth.　　*Uh-oh!*　<u>*Wow!*</u>　*Word!*

1. The insurance company says it isn't going to pay the claim.　*Far out!*　*Bingo!*　*Bummer!*

2. This lottery ticket's got four matching numbers.　*Duh!*　*Gosh!*　*Sweet!*

3. I was thinking about going out for lunch, and then shopping afterwards. Or we could have lunch here and then shop. Or maybe just go to the mall first and then eat when we start to feel hungry. What do you think?　*Wild!*　*Whatever!*　*Gosh!*

4. Sheila's looking a little bit fat. She's not pregnant, is she?　*Awesome!*　*Wow!*　*Bingo!*

5. That cop behind us is flashing his lights. Should we pull over?　*Duh!*　*Yay!*　*Whatever!*

6. I think I just deleted the files you were working on.　*Word!*　*Uh-oh!*　*Wild!*

4 Too Cool for School

Wanna ride?

No, I'm gonna walk.

Gimme one of those hot dogs!

You gotta pay for it first.

Betcha can't hit the bull's-eye.

Lemme try!

Didja pass the test?

I dunno, it was way hard

Many ordinary English words are difficult to spell. Even native speakers of English find spelling difficult! And slang introduces even more spelling possibilities.

When people talk informally, they often join words together, so that you can't tell where one word stops and another begins. Writers sometimes use different spelling to show more clearly how words are actually pronounced. In this book, we call this "slang spelling." (People who study language call it *pronunciation spelling*.)

Here are the explanations of slang spellings from the sentences above:

Wanna ride?
No, I'm gonna walk.

wanna /ˈwɑːnə/ = want to *or* want a
gonna /ˈɡʌnə/ = going to

Gimme one of those hot dogs!
You gotta pay for it first.

gimme /ˈɡɪmi/ = give me
gotta /ˈɡɑːtə/ = got to

Betcha can't hit the bull's-eye.
Lemme try!

betcha /ˈbɛtʃə/ = bet you
lemme /ˈlɛmi/ = let me

Didja pass the test?
I dunno, it was way hard.

didja /ˈdɪdʒə/ = did you
dunno /dəˌnoʊ/ = don't know

GONNA

"Going to" is generally used in two different ways:
1. to mean "traveling to": "I'm going to New York next week."
2. to indicate the future (when followed by a verb): "I'm going to study biology in college."

Gonna is a slang spelling for "going to," but it is only used for the second meaning above. You can say "I'm gonna study biology in college," but not "I'm gonna New York next week."

IMPORTANT: Don't use these spellings when you write papers for school! Use them only when you're writing informally: for example, in an e-mail to a friend, or in a blog. You can also use slang spelling when you're writing down the words someone says:

"I'm gonna kill you!" she shouted.

What happened to "you"?

t-y: We've seen already that the words "what you," in slang pronunciation, sound like /ˈwʌtʃə/ and are sometimes written as **whatcha**.

The same rule applies in other cases where *you* (or another word starting with *y*-) follows a word that ends with a -*t* sound. For example, "bet you," which is pronounced /ˈbɛtʃə/ and sometimes written as **betcha**, and "got you," which is pronounced /ˈgɑːtʃə/ and written as **gotcha**.

Some other word combinations have this same sound but aren't written as a single word:

See if she'll *let ya* drive her car. /ˈlɛtʃə/
You *bet your* life! /ˈbɛtʃɚ/

d-y: When *you* or another word starting with *y*- follows a word that ends in a -*d* sound, the sound change is different. In this case, the sounds change to /dʒ/:

Did ya pass the test? /ˈdɪdʒə/

Writers sometimes use slang spellings, like **didja** for "did you," to show this pronunciation.

Here are some other places where this sound change occurs:

Would ya just shut up for a minute? /ˈwʊdʒə/
They *said your* car was ready. /ˈsɛdʒɚ/
Have you *had your* physical yet? /ˈhædʒɚ/
Did ya eat yet? /ˈdɪdʒə/

Most Americans make this sound change when they talk informally.

Try It!

I. Look at the words and pronunciations in Group 1. They are slang spellings of various word combinations. Choose one of the words for each of the blanks in the sentences in the left-hand column below. Be sure to read your sentence out loud!

GROUP 1	GROUP 2
oughta /ˈɑːtə/ sposta /ˈspoʊstə/ kinda /ˈkaɪndə/ dunno /dəˌnoʊ/ c'mon /kəˈmɑːn/ betcha /ˈbɛtʃə/ didja /ˈdɪdʒə/ hafta /ˈhæftə/ lemme /ˈlɛmi/ lotta /ˈlɑːtə/	on to kind me supposed ought come lot you of don't have did know let bet

EXAMPLE: _____Lemme_____ see whose cars are here.   _____let_____   _____me_____

1. You _____ have your head examined!   _____ _____

2. _____ see the look on his face?   _____ _____

3. We're _____ stay here till they get back.   _____ _____

4. I think you're headed for a _____ trouble.   _____ _____

5. I _____ why he never called me back.   _____ _____

6. Isn't that _____ like cheating?   _____ _____

7. _____ , I haven't got all day.   _____ _____

8. Don't you _____ take the test again?   _____ _____

9. I _____ we get back before they do.   _____ _____

Now look at the words in Group 2, which are the source of the words in Group 1. In the blanks in the right-hand column, write the words that form the word you chose for each sentence in the left-hand column. You can use a word more than once.

II. Circle the words in the sentences below that are affected by a *t-y* or *d-y* sound change. Then read the sentences out loud, using the changed pronunciation.

EXAMPLE: I'll (bet you) he didn't pay for it.

1. Could you wait here a minute?

2. You let your girlfriend use your credit card?

3. Set your stuff down and relax a while.

4. What would your mother do if she caught you?

5. She said you're a lazy bum.

6. Have you got your passport yet?

7. How often should you change the filter?

8. Have you had your last exam yet?

9. It'll bite you if you hold your hand out.

9

Know Your Critters

Critter is an old word related to the word *creature*. People use *critter* informally to refer to any kind of animal, from insects up to large mammals:

"We lifted up the rock and found all these critters underneath it."

"In these woods, the largest critter you're likely to see is a bear."

The names of animals provide many slang words and expressions.

chicken *noun* a coward: "He worried that his friends would call him a chicken."

chicken *adjective* afraid; cowardly: "Carla was too chicken to come with us to the strip club."

chicken out *verb* fail to do something because you're afraid: "Joe chickened out before the fight started."

zebra *noun* a football referee (= game official) who wears a shirt with black and white stripes: "He got thrown out of the game for swearing at the zebra."

weasel *noun* a person you can't trust: "That weasel would say anything to avoid taking responsibility."

weasel out *phrasal verb* avoid a situation or duty: "We made a down payment on the house and now the seller is trying to weasel out."

bear *noun* something very difficult: "It only cost 50 bucks but it was a bear to install."

cow *noun* a fat and annoying woman: "Some cow was blocking three lanes of traffic trying to figure out where to turn." (This word may be offensive, especially to women.)

turkey *noun* a failure; something of very bad quality: "Her last three movies have been turkeys."

dead duck *noun* someone or something that is sure to fail: "That idea was a dead duck from the get-go."

dog *noun* an unattractive person, especially a woman: "He's too vain to go out with someone that everyone thinks is a dog." (Men use this word much more than women, and women may find it offensive.)

mule *noun* a person who secretly carries illegal drugs: "The mules get arrested and the kingpins go scot-free."

snake or **snake in the grass** *noun* a person who deceives or betrays you: "Watch out for him—he's a snake."

skunk *noun* a person you don't like: "His business partner turned out to be a real skunk."

skunk *verb* defeat severely: "Detroit skunked Minneapolis 7-0 in the semifinals."

big fish *noun* a very important person: "They're trying to find a big fish to give the speech."

insect *noun* a worthless person: "She called him an insect and he got up and left the table."

bug *verb* annoy or irritate: "Little things like that don't bug me." If you **bug sb about sth** or **bug sb to do sth**, you pester them in order to make them do something.

worm *noun* a person who you feel contempt for: "Why doesn't she move out on that worm and get her own place?"

pig *noun* **1** someone who eats too much: "Don't be such a pig! Leave some for your little brother." **2** someone who treats other people badly: "She was really a pig to him at the funeral." **3** a policeman: "That's when the pigs showed up and started yelling we were under arrest."

pig or **pig out** *verb*: eat too much: "We pigged out on pizza and then puked afterwards."/ "There was an open buffet and we really pigged."

Try It!

Choose an animal from the following list to fill in the blanks in the sentences below. If the word required is a verb, be sure to write it in the correct tense.

> bear   chicken   cow   dog   cuckoo   duck   fish   fox   goose
> mule   pig   skunk   snake   turkey   weasel   zebra

EXAMPLE: The guy she's dating is such a __*pig*__. He tells her how she compares to his other girlfriends.

1. That was the quarterback's problem and not the fault of the _____.

2. The whole country has gone _____ for low-carb diets.

3. She's a _____ and she'll betray you the minute you turn your back.

4. If he loses this time, you can consider him a dead _____.

5. They were going to flip over a parked police car, but I _____ out and went home.

6. It's a great house, but it's a _____ to keep clean.

7. I tried to run down the escalator but there was this _____ in front of me and I couldn't get around her.

8. It's the worst detective novel I've ever read—a real _____.

9. They lost the first game in overtime and then got _____ in the second one, 20-2.

10. The insurance company is trying to _____ out of paying claims from the flood damage.

11. His last girlfriend was an actress and she was a real _____, but the one he's got now is a _____.

12. Lots of the big _____ have bought land on the island and put up huge houses.

6 How Much Ya Talkin' About?

Many different slang expressions are used to talk about a large number or quantity:

Make that with gobs of ketchup, will you?

Don't worry. We've got loads of time.

Why don't you just fix it with a bunch of duct tape?

I'm sure she'll have a slew of excuses.

I've got a lot of things to tell you

Wow! This is a shitload of laundry.

They must have heaps of money.

I keep getting tons of spam.

SAVE 20% ON FLOWERS !!!

REFINANCE TODAY

EARN OVER $ 100,000 !

When these words are used in the singular, you must use *a* before them (as in three of the examples above). (Most people find **shitload** offensive; see the next unit for more about **shit**.)

When *of* follows any of these words, it's usually pronounced /ə/. If the next word starts with a vowel sound, *of* is pronounced /əv/:

tons of melons /ə/ tons of apples /əv/

Sometimes you'll see slang spellings of "bunch of," "loads of," "lot of," and "lots of":

"Look at that buncha suckers." "They always give out loadsa prizes"
"Sounds like a lotta crap to me." "Lotsa my peeps will be there."

All of these quantity words can be used in the plural (except *slew*) as a one-word answer to a question. These words are usually used to answer "How much" and "How many" questions, but they can also answer yes/no questions about quantity, as in this example.

People sometimes use these quantity words when they don't want to be specific.

Like what? (**Like who?**, **Like where?**, etc.) means that you want more specific information.

"SOME GUY" OR "SOME GUYS"?

In standard English, *some* is most often used with plural nouns ("We looked at some houses") or mass nouns ("We ate some cheese"). But in informal English, **some** is often used like *a* and *an* with singular nouns, and may sound even more indefinite than *a* or *an*: "I read it in some magazine." / "Some idiot stole my parking space." / "Some church is on the phone, asking if we want to give them money."

I. Write sentences that use the following pairs of words. Use your imagination to make up interesting sentences. Be sure to say your sentences out loud.

EXAMPLE: tons/homework _____ *I've got tons of homework to do this weekend.*

1. load/nonsense _____

2. slew/photos _____

3. heaps/trouble _____

4. gobs/money _____

5. ton/food _____

6. loads/time _____

7. bunch/crybabies _____

8. tons/paper _____

II. Write a response to the sentences below using *like* and a question word.

EXAMPLE: Lotsa people said they would be there. _____ *Like who?* _____

1. There's all kinds of places you can buy those. _____

2. We're gonna finish that up a little later. _____

3. It seemed like there were still some boxes left. _____

4. She told me a bunch of crazy stuff. _____

5. I might know a way to get out of here. _____

6. Some girls over there want to talk to you. _____

14

Words Fail Me

What are these people talking about?

What's all that stuff in the back of your car?

Just some junk I picked up at a yard sale.

Did you dump all this crap on the dining room table?

I want your shit out of here by the time I come back.

People use all these words — **stuff**, **junk**, **crap**, and **shit** — as a way to talk about something, or a group of things, that is easier than naming them precisely.

stuff is usually a neutral word. It can be used for almost anything when it's too much trouble to use the real names for it all.

junk is a slightly negative word. It's often used to describe something you think is worthless.

crap is a negative word, and some people find it offensive. People use it to describe things that irritate them.

shit is a negative word. Some people use it to describe things in an annoyed or angry way. You shouldn't say it.

THE S-WORD

Shit has many other meanings that we will discuss later. But even though it's very common, it's usually offensive; you should think carefully before you use it. If you need to talk about the word without saying it, you can call it "the s-word."

15

Stuff, **junk**, **crap**, and **shit** can be used with the quantity words you used in the last unit:

> "There's gobs of stuff the college is giving away free."
> "Somebody left a load of junk in our driveway."
> "Their house is overflowing with tons of crap."

Note that, in these phrases, *of* is pronounced /ə/.

Stuff, **junk**, **crap**, and **shit** are also used to talk about nonmaterial things: feelings, activities, language, or anything else. You only know what they refer to from the context (the conversation or piece of writing that they occur in):

 Isn't there any fun stuff to do here?

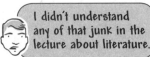 I didn't understand any of that junk in the lecture about literature.

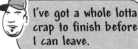 I've got a whole lotta crap to finish before I can leave.

 Leave her alone, she's just dealing with her own shit.

fun stuff to do = fun activities

junk in the lecture = material in the lecture

a whole lotta crap to finish = a lot of work to finish

dealing with her own shit = dealing with her own emotions or feelings

More weasel words

A *weasel word* is a word used by someone who doesn't want to be direct. (Remember what Unit 5 said about weasels.) There are many words that people often use when they don't wish to give you very much information. Many of these words are informal or slang.

How did the interview go?

It was kinda . . . I dunno.

What sorts of questions did they ask?

A buncha stuff. You know, yada yada yada.

Is there a lot of competition for the job?

Kinda. It's like . . . uh. I mean, I guess. Prob'ly.

Do you think you might get the job?

The thing is . . . well . . . um . . . sorta.

We don't learn very much from the guy here, but it's useful to know about some of the expressions he uses.

kinda, sorta You've seen these words before: **kinda** = *kind of* and **sorta** = *sort of*. When people answer a question with **"Kinda"** or **"Sorta,"** it means "Yes in some ways."

yada yada yada People use this expression (or sometimes only **yada yada**) when they're talking about something spoken or written that is obvious or long or boring, so they don't have to tell you the exact words. Another similar expression is **blah blah blah.**

I mean, I guess, It's like, The thing is People sometimes start a sentence with these expressions when they aren't very confident about what they're going to say. These phrases don't add any meaning to sentences. **I guess,** when spoken all by itself, can also mean "I think so."

prob'ly = probably.

Try It!

I. Choose a word from the list that you think is closest to the meaning of the underlined word or words.

EXAMPLE: Was there any <u>stuff</u> to do over the weekend for Biology?
    A. maps   B. meals   (C. homework) D. music

1. I heard some <u>crap</u> about him not coming with us.
    A. lies   B. music   C. bells   D. information

2. We got six more inches of powdery <u>shit</u> last night.
    A. rain   B. snow   C. paper   D. food

3. She puts all kinds of weird <u>junk</u> in her salsa.
    A. peas   B. salt   C. ingredients D. information

4. Have you been to their house? Talk about some top-dollar <u>stuff</u>!
    A. food   B. cars   C. children D. furniture

II. Read the paragraph below, in which a man talks about music that he listens to. Then,

1. Circle all of the words that add no meaning or that aren't specific about anything.

2. Rewrite the paragraph, putting more specific words in place of words such as *guys, stuff,* **and** *junk.*

I kinda like rock music, I just don't like doing it myself, you know? I mean I love the Stones. One of my favorite singers is Bruce Springsteen. But, who else? I don't know. There's a lot of stuff. The Sex Pistols I sorta like — guys like that. The thing is, I don't know that much from earlier. I mean I really don't know any of the dead artists. Except I know Fats Waller and he's amazing. Most of the stuff I listen to now is like ambient or instrumental. I guess I should probably get to know more of those early guys — Frank Sinatra and Dean Martin and guys like that. There's loads of shit I've only heard once or twice that I should probably kinda study or something.

_____

_____

_____

_____

_____

_____

_____

_____

_____

Ka-ching!

A bell rings when the drawer on a cash register opens. **"Ka-ching!"** imitates this sound, and refers to money, especially to spending or making money.

There are many slang terms for money and for the kinds of money:

Dollar; one-dollar bill. Also called **buck**, **clam**, **one**, **smacker**. These words are often used with numbers, and are usually plural.

> "I betcha 50 bucks."
> "It's a nice restaurant if you feel like blowing 40 smackers on lunch."

Five-dollar bill. Also called **fin**, **five**, **fiver**, **five-spot**.

> "You got a five for five ones?"

Ten-dollar bill. Also called **sawbuck**, **ten**, **tenner**, **ten-spot**.

> "I gotta ten-spot that says he ripped off the lyrics."

Hundred-dollar bill. Also called **Ben Franklin**, **C-note**, **hundred**.

> "Why should I blow a C-note on a blind date?"

Other Amounts of Money

$1,000 is a **grand**, a **thou** /ˈθaʊ/, or a **K** (**K** only comes after a number, and **grand** and **thou** often do):

> Our health insurance is costing us ten grand a year.
> She lost a few thou on the deal.
> Just because he makes 150K a year doesn't mean he's smart.

Paper money (instead of coins) can be called **greenbacks**, **dead presidents**, or **folding money**:

> Slip him a few greenbacks and he'll tell you what you want to know.
> She's got a mattress full of dead presidents at home.
> If you want to leave with folding money, you better take lots of it in.

Money in coins is called *change*. **Change** can also mean a small amount of money in addition to a larger amount.

> The house cost them 300 grand and some change. (= a little more than $300,000)

Large amounts of money are described with **wad** or **chunk**:

> Don't go there without a wad of cash to spend.
> He drives a Lexus and always carries around huge wads of money.
> I bet she dropped a chunk of change on that ring.

How much you got?

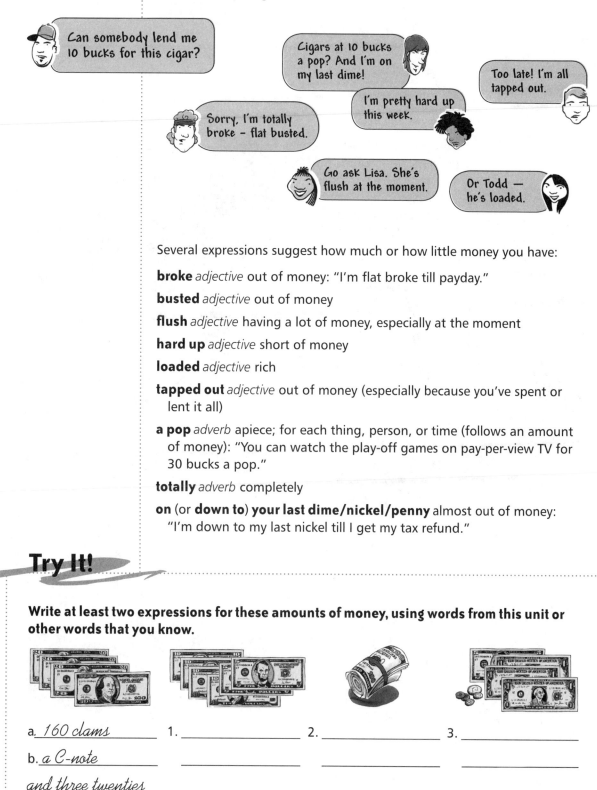

Can somebody lend me 10 bucks for this cigar?

Cigars at 10 bucks a pop? And I'm on my last dime!

Too late! I'm all tapped out.

Sorry, I'm totally broke – flat busted.

I'm pretty hard up this week.

Go ask Lisa. She's flush at the moment.

Or Todd — he's loaded.

Several expressions suggest how much or how little money you have:

broke *adjective* out of money: "I'm flat broke till payday."

busted *adjective* out of money

flush *adjective* having a lot of money, especially at the moment

hard up *adjective* short of money

loaded *adjective* rich

tapped out *adjective* out of money (especially because you've spent or lent it all)

a pop *adverb* apiece; for each thing, person, or time (follows an amount of money): "You can watch the play-off games on pay-per-view TV for 30 bucks a pop."

totally *adverb* completely

on (or **down to**) **your last dime/nickel/penny** almost out of money: "I'm down to my last nickel till I get my tax refund."

Try It!

Write at least two expressions for these amounts of money, using words from this unit or other words that you know.

a. _160 clams_   1. _____   2. _____   3. _____

b. _a C-note_   _____   _____   _____

and three twenties _____   _____   _____

9 Low on Dough?

Dough is one of many different slang words for "money." Here are some slang expressions about spending money and people's attitudes about it:

The chintzy sucker wouldn't even give me cab fare home.

What a tightwad! And after he dropped twenty smackers on a shot of tequila!

Don't be such a cheapskate! She deserves a better tip than that.

Five clams isn't exactly chicken feed.

The bill was $75! A $5 tip on that is chump change.

Tracey's such a gold digger. She always goes for the big spenders.

I heard that her boob job set her back 5,000 bucks.

And that's after she blew a grand on a trip to Vegas.

Why don't you see if Mr. Moneybags over there will buy you a drink?

I'm looking for somebody with really deep pockets, not just a nickel-and-dime lounge lizard.

chintzy *adjective* unwilling to spend money; stingy

nickel-and-dime *adjective* having or involving small amounts of money

big spender *noun* a person who spends a lot of money

cheapskate *noun* a person who avoids spending money

chicken feed *noun* a small amount of money

deep pockets *noun* lots of money

dough /ˈdoʊ/ *noun* money

gold digger *noun* someone who is interested in others mainly for their money

moneybags *noun* a rich person

tightwad *noun* a person who doesn't like to spend money

set sb back *phrasal verb* cost someone

blow *verb* spend

drop *verb* spend

Other vocabulary:

boob job *noun* surgery to make a woman's breasts larger

lounge lizard *noun* a man without much money who spends time in places where he can meet wealthy people

TAKE THAT!

The common verb *take* has many slang meanings that are related to money. If you **take someone for** some amount, or **take someone to the cleaners**, you cheat them out of money or charge them too much:

> The car mechanic just **took us for** a hundred bucks.
> We won the case but the lawyers really **took us to the cleaners**.
> You paid $500 for that? Boy, did you **get taken**!

The take means the amount of money that is made or collected in some situation:

> They want 20% of **the take** from the concert or they say we'll get no protection.

Try It!

I. Fill in the blanks in this telephone conversation with words you have learned in this unit or the previous unit. In many cases, there's more than one suitable answer.

HEATHER: Tiff? Hot news. Jason just gave Whitney an engagement ring.

TIFFANY: You're kidding! Wasn't he supposed to be totally _____?

HEATHER: Well I guess not. The thing _____ him _____ 3,000 bucks.

TIFFANY: Jason _____ three _____ on an engagement ring?

HEATHER: He must've maxed out three credit cards to do it. And knowing him, he _____ _____. He doesn't have the sense to know what things cost.

TIFFANY: I heard his parents are_____ and they'll bail him out if he's in debt.

HEATHER: Well get this: Whitney's already talking about having a wedding reception at the Ritz!

TIFFANY: Either her parents are crazy or they have very _____ _____.

II. Complete these sentences, using your imagination, and then read them out loud.

EXAMPLE: That guy is such a cheapskate that _*he uses paper napkins three times!*_

1. I could tell that she was a gold digger when she_____.

2. Fifty bucks is chump change compared to what they charge you for _____.

3. If I had a wad of cash, the first thing I'd do is _____.

4. How could he say he was broke and then blow a hundred bucks on _____?

5. I'll betcha 50 smackers that _____.

6. The last time I _____ I really got taken to the cleaners.

7. Is that supposed to be_____? Wow! How much did they take you for?

10 Check This Out

You've probably already learned many of the hundreds of phrasal verbs in English. Here's a quick review of the subject:

Phrasal verbs are made from an ordinary verb and another small word — a preposition or an adverb. In a few cases, the ordinary verb is followed by *two* small words. (These small words are often called *particles*.) A phrasal verb's meaning is different from the meaning that the ordinary verb has alone. Phrasal verbs can be transitive (taking an object), intransitive (taking no object), or both.

Transitive:	Children *act out* their fantasies.
Intransitive:	They raise cotton where I *grew up.*
Both:	The police *pulled over* a white van with Missouri license plates.
	I *pulled over* because the engine was smoking.

In the last two sentences, the transitive and intransitive meanings are related. However, many phrasal verbs have transitive and intransitive meanings that aren't related to each other:

The gang *held up* (=robbed) three convenience stores in one night.
This car isn't *holding up* (=lasting) as well as my last one did.

When the object of a transitive phrasal verb is a short word, it may be placed between the verb and the particle. If it's a personal pronoun (*me, it, them,* etc.), it *must* be placed there.

It was dark and I couldn't make out *what was written on the sign.*
It was dark and I couldn't make *it* out.

Phrasal verbs of this type (ones that have a *movable object*) are indicated in this book by a special symbol: **scarf sth ⇄ up**, **wolf sth ⇄ down**.

Slang uses many phrasal verbs that aren't used in standard English. Here are some examples:

All these phrasal verbs are transitive and have a movable object:

blow sb ⇄ away amaze someone

check sth ⇄ out examine or inspect something

hit sb ⇄ up ask someone to give or lend you money

put sb ⇄ down insult someone

Now, an important point: Look at the pronunciation of these verbs with their objects:

　　Our new song really *blew them* away. /'blu:wəm/
　　If you go by that new restaurant, *check it* out, will you? /'tʃɛkət/
　　Why do you always *hit her* up when she's tapped out? /'hɪtɚ/
　　I hate the way she always *puts him* down. /'pʊtsəm/

What's the deal? When do you say these words this way?

The lowdown: These four pronouns, when they are the object of a verb, are pronounced very short in informal speech. Those that begin with a consonant sound lose that sound:

　　him /əm/　　　　her /ɚ/　　　　it /ət/　　　　them /əm/

Rewrite the sentences below in standard English, but change the object to a pronoun and move it. Then say your new sentence out loud, using the pronunciation shown above. You can look up the phrasal verbs you don't know in the index or in a dictionary.

EXAMPLE: She wants to freak out her parents with her new hairstyle.

She wants to freak them out with her new hairstyle.

1. Somebody goofed up the commands and we have to start over again.

   _____

2. You're really going to tick off Mr. Readle if you break off that piece.

   _____

3. If you don't wolf down that pizza we're gonna be late.

   _____

4. They kicked out Marcia Smith because she was never on time.

   _____

5. They ripped off those lawn chairs at a flea market.

   _____

6. I can't believe you were stupid enough to flip off the principal!

   _____

7. Why don't you get together with her and work out the schedule?

   _____

8. He said he picked up that Asian girl at a mall.

   _____

If Ya Can't Beat 'em, Join 'em

You know the English personal pronouns (*I, me, you, he, him, she, her, it, we, us, they, them)*, and you've seen how some of them change their pronunciation in informal speech. In the last unit, you learned how *him, her, it,* and *them* are pronounced informally. *Him, her,* and *them* are sometimes written with slang spellings to show this:

> Our new song really blew 'em away.

> Why do you always hit 'er up when she's tapped out?

> I hate the way she always puts 'im down.

All About You

In Unit B, we saw that when *you* isn't stressed, it's sometimes pronounced /jə/ and written as *ya:* "How ya doin'?"

And don't forget that when *you* follows a *t* sound, the combination of letters is often pronounced /tʃ/. This gives us the slang spelling **whatcha** for "what you."

I'll *let you* off at the corner. /ˈlɛtʃə/
You didn't tell me that a snake *bit you!* /ˈbɪtʃu/ or /ˈbɪtʃə/

When *you* follows a *d* sound, the combination of *d* and *y* is sometimes pronounced /dʒ/.

Did you see the lightning last night? /ˈdɪdʒə/
I *need you* to pick something up for me. /ˈniːdʒə/

You and You: Although *you* is both a singular and plural pronoun, informally people use different forms for the plural.

What're you guys doin' here?

What time did y'all get back?

Have you all eaten yet?

The most common plural forms of *you* are **you guys, you all,** and **y'all. Y'all** is used especially in the American South.

More shortcuts

Two other very common words—*or* and *and*—often get a short pronunciation. *Or* is often pronounced /ɚ/, and *and* is often pronounced /ən/. To indicate this, *and* is sometimes written as *'n'*: "Come 'n' see!"

When *he* occurs in the middle of a sentence, especially after a short word, it loses its *h* sound and gets a very short pronunciation:
    Talk loud *or he* won't hear you. /ɚri/
    If he'd call I could tell him. /ˈɪfid/

Try It!

Read the following sentences out loud. Be sure to use the slang pronunciation for all the underlined words.

1. How <u>did you</u> find <u>them</u> so fast?

2. I <u>told you</u> guys we should've dropped <u>him</u> off first.

3. She asked <u>him</u> if <u>he'd got you</u> a present.

4. Why <u>don't you</u> try to pick <u>her</u> up?

5. <u>Did y'all</u> hear what <u>it</u> costs to bring <u>them</u> back?

6. They're not gonna <u>let you</u> keep <u>him.</u>

7. <u>You</u> should've checked <u>them</u> out before you bought <u>them.</u>

8. I know <u>it'll set you</u> back at least a grand.

9. I <u>said you</u> guys couldn't stay long enough to bail <u>her</u> out.

Sack Time

Are all these new words making you tired?
Maybe you should crash for a while!

I'm totally wiped out. Time to hit the sack!

There's Stuart, catching some Z's on the couch.

Wonderin' about that racket? It's Marcia, sawing logs on the hammock.

And there's Bill, conked out in a deck chair.

Hello? Isn't that Michael crashed out on my bed?

How's a person supposed to get a snooze around here when all the places are taken? I guess I could rack out on the recliner...

...but I wouldn't mind a bite to eat, and here's Michael's cookies! If ya snooze, ya lose!

All right! Beddy-bye for me! Sure can't beat shut-eye!

ZZZ ZZZZZ

Here are some of the many slang expressions related to sleep:

beddy-bye /'bɛdiˌbaɪ/ *noun* the time or the act of going to sleep: "All right, one more game and then it's beddy-bye."

sack time *noun (1)* time to sleep or go to bed *(2)* time spent sleeping: "I haven't been getting enough sack time lately."

shut-eye /'ʃʌtˌaɪ/ *noun* sleep

snooze *noun* a short sleep; a nap

conk out *phrasal verb* sleep; go to sleep (often as adjective: *conked out*)

crash *verb* or **crash out** *phrasal verb* sleep; go to sleep

rack out *phrasal verb* sleep; go to sleep (often as adjective: *racked out*)

snooze *verb* sleep lightly for a short time: "He likes to snooze for a while after lunch."

wipe sb out *phrasal verb* make someone very tired (usually as adjective: *wiped out*)

catch some Z's/shut-eye sleep

hit the sack go to bed

If you snooze you lose If you're not paying attention, you may miss opportunities or others may take an advantage

saw logs snore while sleeping

DID YOU KNOW?

People who draw cartoons write "zzzzz" to show that a person is sleeping or snoring. This is why we say "catch some Z's." Here are some other things you can "catch":

catch some flak/heat be blamed or criticized for something you've done: "She's gonna catch some flak for leaving the office unattended." Some people instead say **catch some shit**, but this can be offensive.

catch some rays lie in the sun; sunbathe: "Let's catch some rays at the beach."

catch some waves go surfing: "I like to get up really early and catch some waves."

You can use *catch* with many other nouns to mean "experience or engage in some activity":

"Let's go over to Jerry's and catch some football." (= watch football on TV)

"Did you happen to catch (= see) Madonna on the Letterman show last night?"

And of course, if you're lucky, you can catch some fish!

Try It!

I. Write sentences about yourself in answer to these questions, using the word or expression in parentheses. Be sure to say your sentences out loud!

EXAMPLE: What time do you go to bed? (hit the sack)

I usually hit the sack about 11 p.m.

1. Do you sleep anywhere besides in your bed? (rack out)

_____

2. How much sleep do you need every night? (sack time)

_____

3. What do you do if you get sleepy during the day? (snooze)

_____

4. Do you go to bed at the same time on weekends as you do during the week? (crash)

_____

5. When do you think is the best time to take a nap? (catch some Z's)

_____

6. Do you think you always have lots of energy? (wipe out)

_____

7. What's your usual schedule on weekends? (shut-eye)

_____

II. Fill in the blanks below with the word from this list that matches the meaning in parentheses.

vids	tracks	pix	plays

1. Let's go down to the beach and catch some _____. (take pictures)

2. We had to leave early and only caught a few _____. (heard songs)

3. They went to New York to catch some _____. (went to the theater)

4. We stayed home last night and caught some _____. (watched movies)

13 You Shoulda Been There!

Some modal verbs (*should, could, would, must,* and *might*) are used with *have* and another verb to talk about things that didn't happen, or probably did happen, in the past:

"You should have gone to bed earlier."
"They could have left us something to eat!"
"We would have beat the traffic if we'd left on time."
"I must have missed the exit."
"I might have left my wallet in the restaurant."

They could have left us something to eat!

I must have missed the exit.

In informal speech, the *ha-* sound of *have* disappears:

"You should've gone to bed earlier!"
"They could've left us something to eat!"
"We would've beat the traffic if we'd left on time."
"I must've missed the exit."
"I might've left my wallet in the restaurant."

They could've left us something to eat!

I must've missed the exit.

In slang speech, if the next word starts with a consonant sound, the *v* sound of *have* disappears instead, and *have* is simply pronounced as /ə/. Slang spelling is sometimes used to show this:

"You shoulda gone to bed earlier!"
"They coulda left us somethin' to eat!"
"We woulda beat the traffic if we'd left on time."
"I musta missed the exit."
"I mighta left my wallet in the restaurant."

They coulda left us somethin' to eat!

I musta missed the exit.

But if the word after *have* starts with a vowel sound, most people pronounce the *v* sound. In the following sentences, the pronunciation of *have* is /əv/:

"We should've eaten before we came."

"I think she might've ODed on heroin."

"The mafia could've iced 'em and tossed 'em in the river."

Is it *have* or *to*?

Two other slang contractions from common verbs end with an /ə/ sound:

hafta /ˈhæftə/ is a slang contraction of *have to*.

gotta /ˈgɑːtə/ is a slang contraction of *got to*.

Hafta and **gotta** often have exactly the same meaning. You use them to talk about something you are required to do.

Mighta and **gotta** are sometimes pronounced with a *d* sound where the *t* is. We'll look at this later.

> I hafta stay here till Jerry gets back.

> No way! You gotta go to the store with me.

WHAT'S THE DEAL? Can you really say "You got to go to the store with me"?

The lowdown: Not when you're speaking standard English. But remember that auxiliary verbs are often dropped in slang sentences. So "You gotta go to the store with me" means "You have got to go to the store with me."

Try It!

Fill in the blanks with one of the words from the list. For some sentences, more than one answer may be correct. Say the sentences out loud. But remember: Don't use these slang spellings in formal writing!

coulda	gotta	hafta	musta	mighta	shoulda	woulda

EXAMPLE: You __*woulda*__ figured it out if you'd thought about it longer.

1. Of course you _____ pay it all. I _____ told you that.

2. You _____ gotten the job if you'd dressed for the interview.

3. Who _____ guessed that they were married all this time?

4. It _____ been nice if you'd warned me they were coming.

5. I can't go, I really _____ study tonight.

6. She _____ got rid of all that stuff; now she's _____ store it.

All Tooled Up

Tools and devices that everyone uses have related slang or informal meanings. All these verbs are related to the action of tools.

ax *(1)* fire: "Two teachers got axed for dating their students."
(2) cancel: "They've axed the rest of the games this season."
(3) remove from a group: "The company axed five branch offices last week."

clamp attach something strongly by using authority: "The judge clamped a restraining order on the girl's father."

clamp down on sb/sth take action to stop or control something: "Why hasn't the government clamped down on Internet pornography?"

fork sth ⇄ over pay or give something, especially when you don't want to: "If you don't fork over the cash by tonight, me and my friends are going to come and get it."

hammer *(1)* defeat severely: "Chicago hammered Miami in the play-offs."
(2) criticize severely: "The boss really hammered me for being late again."

hammer away at sth keep talking about or criticizing something: "The president kept hammering away at his critics."

hook to addict *(usually passive)*: "Her boyfriend got hooked on crack."

hook up with meet someone for a purpose, especially for sex: "Cheryl hooked up with some guy at the bar and I came home alone."

nail *(1)* arrest or convict for a crime: "The cops nailed him for burglary."
(2) do, portray, or recognize something with success and accuracy: "We placed bets on who would win the election, and Joe was the only one who nailed it."

pump *(1)* get or try to get information from someone: "When she gets here, pump her for everything that happened."
(2) put in a large amount of sth: "They pumped me full of antibiotics and sent me home."

ratchet sth ⇄ up move up in small steps: "Every six months they ratchet up my car-insurance rates."

ream *also* **ream sb ⇄ out** *(1)* criticize someone severely: "My dad reamed out me and Aaron for smashing up the car."

(2) defeat severely: "They got reamed in their first game this year."

screw *or* **screw sb over** treat badly or cheat someone: "They screwed us over on the phone bill."

screw have sex with someone (sometimes offensive): "She screwed him in the car in her driveway while her parents were watching TV."

Try It!

Fill in the blanks in the sentences below using a verb from the list, being sure to use the proper tense. Where there are two blanks, use a phrasal verb.

ax   clamp   fork   hammer   hook   nail   pump   ratchet   ream   screw

EXAMPLE: The cops really ___clamped down___ on speeders last weekend.

1. We really got _____ on the tickets because we bought them at the last minute.

2. Why should I _____ _____ a hundred bucks when there's no guarantee I'll get the room?

3. _____ him for all the latest gossip from the dorm.

4. Because of the budget cuts, they had to _____ ten jobs.

5. The newspapers continued to _____ _____ at the governor.

6. Why don't we _____ _____ sometime next week and talk about it?

34

Ain't No Point

Ain't no mountain high enough . . .

What I ain't trying to do is lie to you . . .

You ain't woman enough to take my man . . .

As you know, slang isn't always very strict about grammar. Many rules that are important in standard English are ignored when people speak slang. (Language experts sometimes call this usage *nonstandard* rather than *wrong* or *incorrect*.)

Ain't /eɪnt/ is a good example of a word that is widely used but is considered nonstandard — or incorrect, if you ask some people. **Ain't** is popular because it's short and it can serve as the contraction of several different verb forms with *not*. It can take the place of *am not, are not,* or *is not*:

"Ain't no mountain . . . " = "There isn't any mountain"
"What I ain't trying to do . . ." = "What I'm not trying to do"
"You ain't woman enough . . ." = "You aren't woman enough"

And it can also take the place of *have not* or *has not*:

"She ain't been home all week." = "She hasn't been home all week."
"We ain't eaten since yesterday." = "We haven't eaten since yesterday."

For some speakers, especially African-Americans, **ain't** may even take the place of *do not, does not,* or *did not*:

"It ain't have to be like this." = "It doesn't have to be like this."
"I ain't listen to none of that crap." = "I don't listen to any of that crap."

Almost everyone uses **ain't** in some fixed expressions:

Ain't it the truth? (= Isn't it the truth?) People say this to agree that something disappointing is true.
You ain't seen nothin' yet (= You haven't seen anything yet) In other words, something that will happen in the future is much bigger than something that has already happened.
If it ain't broke, don't fix it (= If it isn't broken, don't fix it) In other words, you shouldn't interfere with something that's working properly.
_____ **it ain't** (= It's not _____) People say this to express a negative judgment: "She manages to hit all the high notes, but opera it ain't."

WHAT'S THE DEAL? Should you use **ain't** when you speak or write?

The Lowdown: In general, no — unless you're using one of the fixed expressions above. It's important to understand how **ain't** works in sentences, but if you use it a lot, people will think you didn't learn English properly. If you're a rapper or a singer, though, **ain't** can be a very handy word!

When people use **ain't,** they often also make a grammatical error called a double negative: that is, using two negative words (such as *no, none, not, never,* or *neither*) in one clause. In slang, these negative words often take the place of *a, any, some, ever,* or *either* to give the same meaning, even though this creates a double negative:

"We don't need no education." = "We don't need any education."
"I ain't got no place to go." = "I haven't got any place to go."
"We never saw no cops." = "We didn't see any police."
"I ain't no genius." = "I'm not a genius."
"You ain't rich enough and I ain't neither." = "You aren't rich enough and I'm not either."

Try It!

Read these sentences out loud, then rewrite them in standard English.

EXAMPLE: She ain't got no class. *She hasn't got any class.*

1. It ain't none of your business._____

2. I ain't goin' noplace. _____

3. There ain't nobody smarter than him. _____

4. He ain't never worked a day in his life. _____

5. She ain't no fashion model._____

6. I ain't gonna let you get away with it. _____

7. They ain't wearin' no clothes. _____

8. It ain't whatcha think it is. _____

16

A Clip Joint

A **clip joint** is a business that cheats its customers by charging them too much. This comes from the slang verb **clip**.

In standard English, the main meaning of *clip* is "cut." When you clip a word, you break it in parts and keep only one. Many words in standard English are clipped forms of longer words, such as *bus* (from *omnibus*), *dorm* (from *dormitory*), and *flu* (from *influenza*).

Clipping is a popular way of making slang words out of longer words, especially if the long word is formal or difficult.

Congrats on the new do! Totally glam!

Thanks. My hairdresser is a wiz.

bud /ˈbʌd/ buddy (male friend)

burbs /ˈbɚbz/ suburbs (residential areas near a city)

carbs /ˈkɑɚbz/ carbohydrates (main nutrient in foods such as bread, potatoes, rice, and pasta)

'cause /ˈkʌz/ because

condo /ˈkɑːndoʊ/ condominium (an apartment owned by the people who live in it)

congrats /kənˈɡræts/ congratulations

Hey bud! Why the tux?

'Cause there's a party at the frat tonight for new grads.

do /ˈduː/ hairdo

fab /ˈfæb/ fabulous

fave /ˈfeɪv/ favorite

frat /ˈfræt/ fraternity (organization for male university students)

glam /ˈɡlæm/ glamorous

grads /ˈɡrædz/ graduates

'rents /ˈrɛnts/ parents

shrooms /ˈʃruːmz/ mushrooms

tux /ˈtʌks/ tuxedo (formal suit)

wiz /ˈwɪz/ wizard

za /ˈzɑː/ pizza

I thought your 'rents lived in the burbs.

Yeah, but they've also got a fab condo on the lake.

Wow! Za with shrooms! My fave!

Not me, I'm trying to cut down on carbs.

Sometimes the clipped part of a word that you keep is pronounced differently than in the original word:

decaf /'diːˌkæf/ decaffeinated coffee

detox /'diːˌtɑːks/ detoxification (treatment program for drug or alcohol addicts)

info /'ɪnfoʊ/ information

limo /'lɪmoʊ/ limousine (a big, expensive car)

'stache /'stæʃ/ mustache

Try It!

Fill in the blanks in the sentences below with a clipped form from this list. In the blank at the end of each sentence, write the word that is the source of the clipped word, which you can find in the list following the sentences. Look up the words that you don't know in a dictionary.

'cept   cred   veggies   fridge   lech   pic   ref   rep   'bout   zine

EXAMPLE: The ____*ref*____ kicked him out of the game for swearing. ____*referee*____

1. How _____ going to the beach this weekend? _____

2. After he got arrested, his _____ went way up with the drug dealers.

   _____

3. There wasn't anybody there _____ three jocks. _____

4. Her uncle's an old _____ who's always trying to paw my leg. _____

5. Who's your _____ in Congress? _____

6. E-mail me a _____ so I'll recognize you when we meet. _____

7. Check and see if there's any _____ in the _____.

   _____   _____

   lecher   about   vegetables   except   credibility   representative   picture
   magazine   referee   reputation   magazine   refrigerator

38

17

Yer Yankin' My Chain

Who's convinced and who's not?

People use different slang expressions to show that they believe or agree with what someone is saying:

    "Amen!"   "Damn straight!"   "I heard that!"

    "I hear ya!"   "Right on!"   "Word!"

IT MAKES A DIFFERENCE!

Amen is the word that Christians and Jews say at the end of a prayer or hymn. For this meaning it is usually pronounced /ɑˈmɛn/. **Amen** is also used to show that you agree strongly with what someone has said. For this meaning, the pronunciation /ˈeɪˈmɛn/ is usually used.

Many slang words are used to describe speech or writing that you don't believe or don't agree with. These words are not polite but sometimes they are used humorously:

baloney /bəˈloʊni/

bullshit (offensive), **bull**

bunk, **bunkum** /ˈbʌŋkəm/

claptrap /ˈklæpˌtræp/

They loved the speech. I bet I'll be president one day.

Horsefeathers!

crap, **crapola** /ˌkræpˈoʊlə/ (both rude)

(a) crock

hogwash /ˈhɑːgˌwɑːʃ/

hooey /ˈhuːwi/

horseshit (often offensive), **horsefeathers**

humbug /ˈhʌmˌbʌg/

malarkey /məˈlɑɚki/

All of these words except **crock** can be used alone to show that you don't agree at all with what someone has just said, or that you think there is no truth in it.

These words are also used in sentences, especially with *give:*

"I've never heard such crap before."

"Don't give me that bullshit!"

"She gave us a lot of hooey about how she didn't have the cash."

"Did you read the press release? It's a total crock."

"All I got out of the lawyer was a bunch of claptrap."

All of these words except **crock** can also be used after "load of" for emphasis:

"That's a load of **baloney/hooey/bullshit/humbug**/etc."

Notice that *of* often gets the informal "uh" pronunciation in these expressions: load of = /ˈloʊdə/

DID YOU KNOW?

In standard English, a *crock* is a large, heavy container used for storing food. From this, the offensive expression **crock of shit** developed, to talk about speech or writing that is mostly lies:

"The committee report is nothing but a crock of shit."

Now people say that something is a **crock** when they don't believe any of it. This expression may be considered slightly rude.

To show that you disagree with or don't believe someone in a more polite way, there are several slang expressions:

You're pulling my leg!

You're yanking my chain!   Come on!

You're putting me on!

You've got to be kidding!

Expressions that would be considered rude are sometimes said in a humorous way to show that you don't believe someone:

Get outta town!

Get outta here!

Shut up!

18 Got Wheels?

Many slang words and expressions are related to cars and driving:

beater *noun* an old car in bad repair

bomb /'bɑːm/ *noun* an old car in bad repair

clunker *noun* an old car in bad repair

hooptie *noun* an old car in bad repair

ride *noun* a car

rust bucket *noun* an old car in bad repair

ride shotgun ride in the front passenger seat of a car or truck

tranny *noun* transmission (the part of a car that changes gears)

wheels *noun* a car

total *verb* completely wreck a car, so it is not worth repairing

punch it drive a car fast by pushing on the accelerator = **step on it**

step on it = **punch it**

Other vocabulary:

dibs *noun* a claim on the use of something: "Anybody got dibs on that piece of cake?"

unload *verb* get rid of something

Here goes used to tell others that you're starting something

hoof it walk

DID YOU KNOW?

Before there were cars, people traveled in coaches, which were often attacked by robbers. To protect the passengers, a man with a shotgun rode next to the stagecoach driver. When you **ride shotgun** you sit next to the driver. Sometimes this spot is simply called **shotgun**.

Nicknames for cars

Some cars and motorcycles have informal names that everyone uses:

BEAMER, BEEMER
(BMW)

CADDY
(CADILLAC)

ROLLS
(ROLLS ROYCE)

HOG
(HARLEY-DAVIDSON)

JAG
(JAGUAR)

CHEVY /ˈʃɛvi/
(CHEVROLET)

OLDS
(OLDSMOBILE)

Try It!

Each sentence in column A below belongs with a sentence in column B. Match up the sentences that belong together, and write the correct number in each blank. Then say all the sentences out loud. Or read a sentence in column A and have your friend find the correct match in column B.

A

1. Who's that riding shotgun with Craig in the Beemer? _____

2. What kind of a ride has he got? _____

3. Wanna give me a ride to the gym? _____

4. Need a lift? _____

5. Let's grab some grub before the movie. _____

6. Is this really as fast as this rust bucket will go? _____

7. Do cops ride hogs? Somebody's coming up on us fast. _____

8. Did you hear? Whitney wrecked her Dad's Caddy and now she has to drive her mom's old beater. _____

9. Can't this clunker do any better than 40 miles an hour? _____

B

1. Bummer! We were supposed to go to the beach this weekend.

2. Can't. The 'rents have got the wheels.

3. I think he drives a Jag.

4. Nah, I'd rather hoof it — I need the exercise.

5. No, but hang on: here goes!

6. Not when there's a cop in a cruiser right behind me.

7. OK, but we'd better step on it or there won't be time.

8. That would be Charlotte, his new squeeze.

9. Is it too late to unload all these empty beer cans?

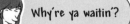

Howdja Do?

Informal speech contains many contractions. You may have already learned or heard many of these:

Why're ya waitin'?

How've ya been?

I wish they'd shut up.

In earlier units we saw some contractions that often have slang spellings, such as **whatcha** (= what you, what are you, what have you), **lotsa** (= lots of), **shoulda** (= should have), and **didja** (= did you), showing more accurately how the words are pronounced.

But there's more! When people speak slang, many different short words can be contracted, sometimes more than one in a sentence. These contractions aren't taught as part of standard English.

Why'd ya do it?

Who'd ya go out with last night?

Where'd he go?

How'd ya find me here?

You've learned that -'d can stand for either *had* (as in "If I'd known I would've come") or *would* (as in "I'd buy it if I were you"). But in the sentences above, -'d stands for *did,* as it usually does when it comes at the end of a question word. When -'d stands for *had* or *would,* it usually comes at the end of a pronoun, not a question word:

I'd = I had *or* I would
they'd = they had *or* they would

Be careful with *who'd.* Since *who* is both a question word and a pronoun, *who'd* can stand for *who had, who did,* or *who would.*

The *'d* has the same pronunciation in each case, so you have to analyze the sentence to know whether it stands for *did, had,* or *would.*

why'd /'waɪd/
how'd /'haʊd/
where'd /'weə˞d/
who'd /'huːd/

Remember that when *y* follows a *d* sound, the combination is pronounced /dʒ/:

"*Why'd ya* do it?" /ˈwaɪdʒə/
"*How'd ya* find me here?" /ˈhaʊdʒə/
"*Who'd ya* go out with last night?" /ˈhuːdʒə/

You'll sometimes see slang spellings of these combinations, like **howdja** (= how did you), but these spellings aren't common.

Try It!

Read these sentences out loud, paying close attention to the pronunciation of the underlined words. Then write the standard English equivalent of these sentences.

EXAMPLE: How'd ya know they'd be here?

How did you know they would be here?

1. Why'd ya let your hair get so long?

_____

2. I didn't think you'd wanna talk to her.

_____

3. Why'd ya gimme only five bucks?

_____

4. Who'd ya say got your tickets?

_____

5. I need ya to do lotsa stuff. _____

6. How'd ya see them from that far away?

_____

7. He'd help if you'd just give him a chance.

_____

8. We'd have stayed if we'd got your message.

_____

9. How'd you know he was gonna bomb?

_____

10. Where'd ya get your new laptop?

_____

20 When Ya Gotta Go . . .

Where's your john? I've gotta pee.

Down the hallway, but somebody's in there takin' a crap.

Why's Mark taking a leak on your flower beds?

Hey! What's the big idea?

Sorry, somebody was usin' the head inside.

Couldn't you wait instead of pissing in my garden?

Looks like the bathroom's free now.

You mean it was only Fluffy?

Cats have to poop too, you know!

People use different words to talk about what you do in the toilet. Almost all of these words are informal or slang; some are offensive.

poop *noun & verb* (used by everyone)

crap *noun & verb* (may be offensive)

shit *noun & verb* (offensive)

take a poop/crap/shit/dump

pee *noun & verb* (used by everyone)

piss *noun & verb* (offensive)

tinkle *noun & verb* (used by children)

take a leak/pee/piss

People also use slang words to talk about the bathroom and the toilet:

can

crapper (may be offensive)

head

john

potty (used by little children)

shitter /ˈʃɪtəˌ/ (offensive)

throne

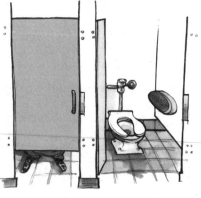

You may have already learned some polite expressions that people use to say they need to use the toilet. Some slang ways of saying this are:

"I gotta go."   "I gotta go bad."   "I'm about to pee my pants."

Nail That Sucker!

You learned earlier (in Unit 7) about words that people use to talk about groups of things, or things that are uncountable, when they don't want to use the real name—especially **stuff**, **junk**, **crap**, and **shit** (offensive). All of these words are noncount nouns: they don't have a plural, and you use *some* or *any* with them rather than *a* or *an*.

To talk about a countable thing that you don't have a proper name for, you can use a different group of slang words.

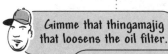

Gimme that thingamajig that loosens the oil filter.

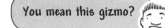

You mean this gizmo?

Some of the most common words for a tool, appliance, or other device whose name you don't know are:

doodad /'duːˌdæd/

gadget /'gædʒət/

gizmo /'gɪzmoʊ/

thingamabob /'θɪŋəməˌbɑːb/

thingamajig /'θɪŋəməˌdʒɪg/

thingy /'θɪŋi/

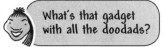

What's that gadget with all the doodads?

Gadget and **gizmo** are normally used for little mechanical objects that have some purpose. A **doodad**, **thingamabob**, **thingamajig**, or **thingy** is usually a small manmade object or a part of a bigger object.

Another useful noun is **sucker**:

Those suckers waiting for tickets are going to be disappointed. The concert sold out online.

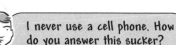

I never use a cell phone. How do you answer this sucker?

I can't believe the cops in this town! That sucker just wrote me a parking ticket!

Sucker has several meanings, but its main slang meanings are (1) a person who is easy to deceive, (2) a person who annoys you, and (3) any person or thing.

Sucker is also a verb, which is often followed by *in* or *into*. It means "deceive."

"The media are completely suckered by this administration."
"How did you get suckered into buying a fur coat?"
"Some investment guy suckered her in and she lost all her savings."

WHAT A DOG!

A word that some people use instead of **sucker** is **bitch**. **Bitch** is usually offensive. Originally, the word meant simply a female dog. But **bitch** is now usually used to mean a difficult woman or a difficult situation or experience: "The calculus quiz was a real bitch." People now often use **bitch** like **sucker**, in place of the name of some other thing: "As soon as I got into that bitch I knew it was the car I wanted to buy." (Even when it's used in this way, it can still be offensive.)

Try It!

Choose the sentence that makes sense for each of the speakers in these pictures, and write its letter in the picture. Be sure to read the sentences out loud!

Get this crap out of here!

1.

2.

3.

Want any of this junk?

4.

5.

Isn't there some doodad you have to push first?

6.

A. I can't get this sucker started.
B. Don't throw out that gadget that I use to catch spiders.
C. I can't go out—I got suckered into babysitting my little brother.
D. What's this thingy for?
E. It's not my stuff, it's Dave's.
F. Get that sucker's license number—he just dented my car!

The Grim Reaper

Slang can be helpful when you have to talk about subjects that are awkward or embarrassing. **The grim reaper** is an expression that people use, usually humorously, to refer to death.

Jerry? This dog's puking on the carpet.

Really? Be right there.

Hey Jerry. The dog's really sick. Now he's got the runs.

I'm coming.

Jerry. Get in here. He's gone belly-up now. I think he's passed out.

I think he popped his clogs.

Bummer. He totally bought the farm.

There are various slang expressions for illnesses and death:

the runs *noun* diarrhea; liquid poop

puke *verb* vomit. Other expressions for this are **barf**, **hurl**, and **toss your cookies**. **Puke** and **barf** are also nouns.

pass out *phrasal verb* faint; lose consciousness (sometimes as a result of drugs or alcohol)

buy the farm die

pop your clogs die. Other expressions that mean "die" include **kick the bucket** and **shit the bed** (offensive).

GO BELLY-UP

Did you ever see a dead fish in the water? Dead fish usually float upside down, with their bellies up. Although this idiom sometimes means "die," it more often means "fail" (for a business) or "stop working" (for a machine): "She sent me a link to a Web site that had already gone belly-up."

Other slang terms describe things that have failed or stopped working:

I have a bad feeling that my computer is about to crap out on me.

My sleep schedule is completely out of whack.

Uh-oh. Looks like the fridge is kaput.

We gotta walk. The motorcycle's all fucked up.

kaput *adjective* useless; no longer working

fucked up *adjective* completely confused or damaged (offensive)

THE F-WORD

Fuck is one of the most offensive words in English. In spite of this, it's also one of the most common words, and it has many uses in slang. You should never have to say **fuck**, but it's important to understand the different ways the word is used. If you need to talk about it without saying it, you can call it "the f-word." If you want to say that someone used a form of **fuck**, you can say that they **dropped an f-bomb**.

crap out (on sb) *phrasal verb* stop working properly

out of whack not working properly

All of the slang expressions that mean "die" can be used about machines and other things that stop functioning completely:
    "It looks like the lawn mower has finally kicked the bucket."
    "Her Volkswagen popped its clogs while she was driving on the highway."

Try It!

I. Write responses to the sentences below, using the word or expression at the end of the sentence. Be sure to read your answers out loud.

EXAMPLE: I thought you had cable service at home. *(crap out)*

I did, but it crapped out on me last week.

1. Why are you using a typewriter? *(out of whack)*

_____

2. Where's Jason going so fast? *(the runs)*

_____

3. Do you feel OK? *(hurl)*

_____

4. Does old man Feeser still live around here? *(pop his clogs)*

_____

5. Why'd you leave in the middle of the lecture? *(puke)*

_____

6. What happened to Cindy? All of her stuff's here. *(pass out)*

_____

7. You didn't answer on your cell phone. What happened? *(kaput)*

_____

8. You got a new TV? What's that about? *(buy the farm)*

_____

II. Only one of the two expressions in parentheses below makes sense in this story. Cross out the one that is wrong, then read the passage out loud.

When I came into Grandpa's room he was *(crapping out/puking)* on his tray. I tried to call the nurse but the phone was *(out of whack/hoofing it)*. I *(hoofed it/punched it)* out into the hallway to find someone. A doctor finally came, but by then it was too late: the old man had already *(bought the farm/put on the feedbag)*.

23 Scope This

You checked out some phrasal verbs in Unit 10. Here are a few more:

bail out leave a bad situation

bum sb ⇄ out make someone unhappy or disappointed

cave in stop opposing or resisting something

chill out relax by doing something quiet, especially alone; calm down

flip out become extremely angry; lose control of oneself

freak sb ⇄ out surprise or frighten someone so much that they can't react reasonably

When **freak out** doesn't have an object, it means "become very excited" or "lose control of yourself." **Freak** can also be used without *out:* "Bob's gonna freak when he sees what you did to his car."

A verb with almost the same meaning is **wig out**, which, like **freak out**, can be used with or without an object: "This girl showed up wearing almost nothing and really wigged me out." "My parents kinda wigged out because Dan got me a ticket to Mexico as an Easter present." Like **freak**, **wig** can be used without *out:* "Max is totally wigged because I think his little brother is a hottie."

Here are a few more common phrasal verbs:

hang out spend time in a place, especially with other people

pump sb ⇄ up make someone feel very happy, proud, or enthusiastic

tick sb ⇄ off make someone angry

These and a few others are sometimes used without the small word at the end. Here are some examples:

bail out → bail: "It looked like it was going to rain so we just bailed."

bum out → bum: "They were really bummed that there were no more tickets left."

cave in → cave: "I wasn't going to spend the money, but when she started crying at the cash register I caved."

chill out → chill: "Why don't we just stay home this evening and chill?"

flip out → flip: "You're gonna flip when I tell you this."

hang out → hang: "Why do you hang with those creeps?"

pump up → pump: "Our finals are over and we're really pumped for vacation."

tick off → tick: "Don't talk to him now, he's really ticked."

Piss off (sometimes offensive) has the same meaning as **tick off**, and **piss** can be used without *off:* "Why's she so pissed?"

You've already learned **pig out**. **Pig** can also be used without *out*: "We totally pigged at the wedding reception."

Finally, **scope sb/sth ⇄ out** means almost the same thing as **check sb/sth out**, but when you **scope out**—or just **scope**—people or things, it usually means you're looking at them for some later purpose: "We scoped the concert hall to see how many seats it had."

Try It!

Write a slang version of these sentences, using one of the verbs on the previous page (without the short word!). To make it easier, parts of some sentences have been filled in. Be sure to read your new sentences out loud.

EXAMPLE: What has made her so angry? Why's she so ____*ticked?*____

1. Don't give in as a result of the children screaming.

   _____ just 'cause the kids are screaming.

2. The team is depressed because they were badly defeated.

   _____ 'cause they got totally whopped.

3. Where did you spend time while you were there?

   Where'd ya _____

4. She's completely happy about the large amount of money she made.

   _____

5. When I want to relax I go to my parents' house in the suburbs.

   _____

6. Why don't you inspect the restaurant to see if it has any attractive qualities?

   _____ to see if it's any good?

7. You should have walked away when he became very angry.

   _____

8. He became extremely upset when he saw how much food they were eating.

   _____

You mighta watched where you were going!

Sorry. I was kinda in a hurry.

You coulda broken my leg!

I was totally outta time.

You oughta be more careful!

You were sorta standing in the middle of the road.

What was I sposta do? Disappear?

You gotta look both ways before crossing the street. You musta known that.

You woulda got a ticket if the police had seen you.

No thanks! I've already got a lotta tickets!

You've already learned (in Unit 13) about modal verbs that form slang contractions with *have*: **coulda**, **woulda**, **shoulda**, **mighta**, and **musta**.

You also learned a few contractions that are formed when *to* follows certain verbs: **wanna** (for *want to*), **gotta** (*got to*), **hafta** (*have to*), and **sposta** (*supposed to*). Another contraction in this group is **oughta** /ˈɑːtə/ = ought to: "You oughta be more careful."

Gotta, **oughta**, and **wanna** are common slang spellings. **Hafta** and **sposta** are less common, but their pronunciations are very common in slang speech.

The conversation above uses another group of slang contractions: contractions formed with *of*. You've already seen most of these:

buncha /ˈbʌntʃə/ = bunch of
kinda /ˈkaɪndə/ = kind of
loadsa /ˈloʊdzə/ = loads of
lotsa /ˈlɑːtsə/ = lots of
lotta /ˈlɑːtə/ = lot of
outta /ˈaʊtə/ = out of
sorta /ˈsoɚtə/ = sort of

In slang speech, these all have the same sound at the end—that is, /ə/. The /v/ sound in *of* and *have* disappears when the next word begins with a consonant sound.

The "uh" sound

Get the picture? There are three important groups of slang contractions that have the same sound at the end. We call this the "uh" sound, because the word "uh" has about the same pronunciation: either /'ʌ/ or /ə/, depending on whether you stress it or not. It's important to hear these sounds when people speak slang and to understand them correctly. How can you tell them apart?

1. The modal verbs *could, might, should, would,* and *must* are never followed by *to* or *of,* so the "uh" sound after these verbs always stands for *have:*

coulda /'kʊdə/ (= could have) "I coulda sworn I saw you here yesterday."

shoulda /'ʃʊdə/ (= should have) "You shoulda kicked his butt."

woulda /'wʊdə/ (= would have) "It woulda been great if we'd gotten here on time."

mighta /'maɪtə/ (= might have) "She mighta won if she'd tried harder."

musta /'mʌstə/ (= must have) "He musta thought I was crazy."

2. The verbs *have, got, ought, supposed,* and *want* are never followed by *have* or *of,* so the "uh" sound after these verbs always stands for *to:*

hafta /'hæftə/ (= have to) "Hooray! I don't hafta work tomorrow!"

gotta /'gɑːtə/ (= got to) "You gotta see this."

oughta /'ɑːtə/ (= ought to) "This oughta be interesting."

sposta /'spoʊstə/ (= supposed to) "What time are we sposta be there?"

wanna /'wɑːnə/ (= want to) "Wanna go for a ride?"

3. Most of the words that are used with *of (bunch of, loads of, lot of, lots of, out of)* are followed by a noun or a noun phrase. Unlike the other two types of "uh" words, these words never come at the end of a sentence.

buncha /'bʌntʃə/ (= bunch of) "She left with a buncha guys an hour ago."

loadsa /'loʊdə/ (= loads of) "That store's got loadsa stuff for under ten bucks."

lotta /'lɑːtə/ (− lot of) "He doesn't act like he's got a lotta brains."

lotsa /'lɑːtsə/ (= lots of) "He tells lotsa jokes and no one laughs."

outta /'aʊtə/ (= out of) "You must be outta your mind."

However, *kind of* and *sort of* (which mean the same thing) can be followed by many different words, or no words:

kinda /ˈkaɪndə/ (= kind of) "She kinda figured we didn't like her."
"I feel kinda weird doing this on the boss's couch."
"What kinda dog is that?"
"Are you tired?" "Kinda."

sorta /ˈsoɚtə/ (= sort of) "Isn't this sorta like stealing?"
"He's been sorta dating a girl."
"That music is sorta loud, isn't it?"
"Is she pretty?" "Yeah, sorta."

Remember: Don't use slang spellings when you write formally! They are okay only when you are writing informal English.

Try It!

Fill in each blank with one of the words shown here. In the blanks at the end of the sentence, write in the full form of each word you have chosen.

coulda gotta hafta kinda loadsa lotsa lotta mighta musta
oughta outta shoulda sorta sposta wanna woulda

EXAMPLE: The test was __*kinda*__ long but the questions were easy.

1. They're _____ dull green and have _____ bumps. _____ _____

2. He started acting _____ weird and then ran _____ the room. _____ _____

3. Mike Tyson at his peak _____ beat anyone!!! _____

4. I don't think Kevin Costner _____ worked in the Ed Harris role. _____

5. Do you _____ play that thing so loud or am I _____ wear earplugs? _____

6. You _____ known they would go in if the door was open. _____

7. It was _____ cool. We learned _____ good stuff. _____ _____

8. We're _____ the bean soup. You _____ try something else? _____ _____

9. Don't you think you _____ go a little slower? _____

10. You _____ seen the look on her face. _____

11. He gave me a _____ books to read. _____

12. We're _____ meet them here but they _____ changed their minds. _____ _____

13. There's no one home; they _____ left earlier. I wish I _____ talked to them before they left. _____ _____

14. They started offering me _____ money. What else was I _____ do except take it? _____ _____

15. If you _____ win, you _____ play the game. _____ _____

Great Bod!

Bod is slang for *body*. People often say "Great bod!" about a man who is muscular or a woman with a nice figure.

All the parts of the body have slang names. But be careful—some of these names are only used when some other idea is involved!

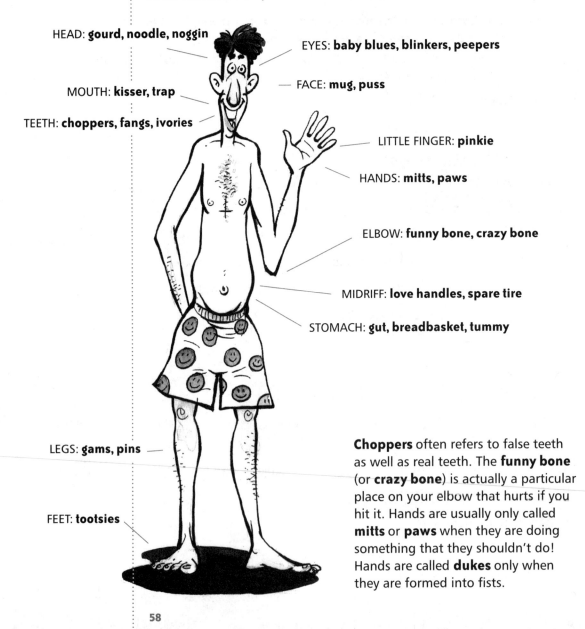

HEAD: **gourd, noodle, noggin**

EYES: **baby blues, blinkers, peepers**

FACE: **mug, puss**

MOUTH: **kisser, trap**

TEETH: **choppers, fangs, ivories**

LITTLE FINGER: **pinkie**

HANDS: **mitts, paws**

ELBOW: **funny bone, crazy bone**

MIDRIFF: **love handles, spare tire**

STOMACH: **gut, breadbasket, tummy**

LEGS: **gams, pins**

FEET: **tootsies**

Choppers often refers to false teeth as well as real teeth. The **funny bone** (or **crazy bone**) is actually a particular place on your elbow that hurts if you hit it. Hands are usually only called **mitts** or **paws** when they are doing something that they shouldn't do! Hands are called **dukes** only when they are formed into fists.

Words that are used for *head* often also mean what is inside it. So some expressions use these words when they really mean "mind" or "brain."

bake your noodle be extremely difficult to understand

bored out of your gourd very bored

use your head/noggin/noodle think: "The questions are easy if you just use your noodle."

have a good head on your shoulders be a smart or sensible person

Parts of the body that are involved in sex have many slang names.

The doctor's word: breasts

Words that children use: **boobs, boobies**

Word that many people use in conversation: **boobs**

Words that men use privately (offensive to women): **headlights, hooters, jugs, knockers, rack, tits**

Any other words to describe women's breasts that you may hear are probably offensive to everyone.

The doctor's word: buttocks

Words that children use: **behind, bottom, fanny** (American English only!)

Words that many people use in conversation: **backside, behind, bottom, buns, butt, heinie, keister, rear, rear end, rump, tush**

Words that men or women use privately (may be offensive): **ass, booty, butt-cheeks**

Any other words for buttocks that you may hear are probably offensive to everyone.

box, cunt, muff, pussy, twat

cock, dick, johnson, pecker, prick, schlong, putz

Slang words for men's and women's sexual organs are never used in polite conversation. All of these words are either embarrassing or offensive to some people. Some words for a man's organ are considered humorous, but those for women are used mainly by men and are very offensive to women.

Try It!

I. Identify what part of the body each of the underlined slang words refers to, and write the standard English word in the blank space. Do not look back at the pictures earlier in this unit!

EXAMPLE: It's easy if you just use your noggin. _____*mind*_____ .

1. Put up your <u>dukes</u> and fight like a man! _____

2. Shut your <u>trap</u> and listen to what I'm saying. _____

3. She only has to wink those gorgeous <u>peepers</u> and he'll do anything she says. _____

4. I was standing in line for hours and my <u>tootsies</u> are tired. _____

5. Keep your <u>mitts</u> off of those cookies! _____

6. How many times has Michael Jackson had plastic surgery on his <u>beak</u>? _____

7. He looks funny when he doesn't have his <u>choppers</u> in. _____

8. She walked into class with a huge grin on her <u>kisser</u>. _____

9. We were only in the car five minutes and his <u>paws</u> were all over me! _____

II. Choose a word from this list that will fit the sentences below. Be sure to read the sentences out loud when you are finished!

baby blues   boobs   gourd   gut   ivories   pinkie   pins   schnoz   tootsy   tush

EXAMPLE: He only turned his back so the chicks could check out his _____*tush*_____ .

1. When he smiles, you can see he's got a few _____ missing.

2. He's a chowhound with a huge _____ and he doesn't exercise.

3. They've got her on so many meds that she's out of her _____ most of the time.

4. Stop sniffling and just wipe your _____ .

5. He dipped one _____ in the water and said it was too cold.

6. She wears a ring on her _____ with a huge diamond in it.

7. I keep getting e-mails that tell me I can have bigger _____ .

8. I looked him right in his _____ and said "No way."

9. She's not too steady on her _____ since the hip replacement.

60

26 By the Numbers

In Unit 6 you learned a bunch of slang words that represent quantities: **loads, slew, heaps, gobs, tons, bunch, lots.**

Some other slang words stand for quantities and are based on numbers. You probably already know the expressions *a couple of* (= about two), *half a dozen* (= about six), and *dozen* (= twelve or about twelve):

Mr. Smith is away from the office for a couple of days.

I've seen that flick at least half a dozen times.

There's a pileup of about a dozen cars on the interstate.

Note that *of* often gets the "uh" pronunciation in the expression *couple of* when the next word starts with a consonant sound:

a couple of minutes /ˈkʌplə/   a couple of hours /ˈkʌpləv/

Several other slang words take the place of different numbers. The number zero has the most slang synonyms:

This baby goes from nada to 60 in just five seconds!

What's up?

Zip.

That guy knows zilch about computers.

I can't see squat without my glasses.

Zip, **zilch**, **nada**, and **squat** are all slang for *zero* or *nothing*. **Zip**, **zilch**, and **squat** can also take the place of *anything* when *anything* is used with a negative word:

"He can't see squat without his glasses." = He can't see anything without his glasses.

"She won't give you zilch for that." = She won't give you anything for that.

"That doesn't mean zip to me." = That doesn't mean anything to me.

Unlike *nothing*, **zip**, **zilch**, and **squat** don't count as negatives, so you don't create a double negative when you use these words with *not*.

Umpteen and **umpteenth** are used when you mean a large number but can't say exactly how large.

> I've told you umpteen times to take out the trash!

> My dad's office is on the umpteenth floor.

For really big numbers, you can use **zillion** or words based on it:

> They won a gazillion bucks in the lottery.

> There were a kazillion questions on the exam.

> We got bitten by a zillion mosquitoes.

> He always takes a bazillion pictures.

Try It!

Choose one word or expression from group A and one from group B, and write a sentence. Write 10 sentences in all. Be sure to read them out loud.

GROUP A
couple of, diddly, gazillion, half a dozen, nada, squat, umpteen, umpteenth, zilch, zillion, zip

GROUP B
clunkers, C-notes, doodads, excuses, hours, learn, meds, pay, times, understand, visit, win

EXAMPLE: _I learned zip in that class the whole semester._

_____

_____

_____

_____

_____

_____

_____

_____

_____

What the heck is that?

Darned if I know.

Let's get the hell out of here.

RRIIIIINNNG!!!

You scared the crap out of me!

I'll be danged if I didn't bash my finger!

Poor dear. It must hurt like the dickens.

People use many extra words in fixed expressions to add emphasis when they're speaking informally. The words don't add meaning to sentences; instead, they simply show the attitude of the speaker.

Danged if, **darned if**, **damned if**, **heck if**, and **hell if** are sometimes used before a negative statement to make it positive, or to express surprise or annoyance. Using **hell if** usually shows that the speaker is angry or out of patience; you shouldn't use it. For some people, **damned** is also offensive.

"I'll be darned if he didn't go right back in." (= He went right back in)
"Hell if I know." (= I don't know) **Heck if I know** is more polite.
"Damned if there weren't 50 people there." (= There were 50 people there)

When people say **I'll be darned/damned** in response to something, it just means that they are surprised ("Look at that monster crowd! — "Well, I'll be damned!").

The heck, **the dickens** (old-fashioned), **the hell** (sometimes offensive), **the crap** (sometimes offensive), **the bejesus** (sometimes offensive), and **the fuck** (offensive) are added after question words to show that the speaker is surprised, confused, or angry:

"How the hell did you get in here?"
"Who the heck took my keys?"
"What the dickens is making that noise?"

Like the devil (slightly old-fashioned), **like the dickens** (old-fashioned), and **like hell** (sometimes offensive) are used to add emphasis:

"We ran like hell but they still caught up to us." (= We ran very fast)
"It rained like the devil for three days." (= It rained heavily)
"We worked like the dickens and finished before dark."
(= We worked very hard)

After certain verbs, **the heck out of**, **the hell out of**, **the crap out of**, **the bejesus out of**, and **the shit out of** are used for strong emphasis.

"Let's just bomb the hell out of them." (= bomb them heavily)
"Two guys just beat the crap out of him." (= beat him up badly)
"That movie'll scare the bejesus out of you." (= scare you a lot)

I hate this job.

Yeah, well, it beats the hell out of being broke.

All of the phrases above are used after *beat* to add emphasis in two expressions:

sth beats sth else one thing is much better than another thing: "Chemistry is a little boring, but it sure beats math!"

(it) beats me I don't know *or* I don't understand: "Why is she always 30 minutes late?" "Beats me."

Why the heck was she carrying so much?

Beats the crap out of me.

THE F-WORD: A BAD SUBSTITUTE

You will hear **fuck** in many of the phrases above (in place of **heck**, **hell**, **crap**, etc.), as well as many other kinds of phrases:

"Fuck if I know" *or* "Beats the fuck out of me." (= I don't know)
"Shut the fuck up." (= Shut up)
"Get the fuck out of my cab." (= Get out of my cab)
"What the fuck do you want?" (= What do you want?)

However, if you use it yourself, people will think that you're angry, rude, and poorly educated.

Try It!

Rewrite the sentences below, inserting an expression that contains the word in parentheses. Read your sentences out loud!

EXAMPLE: Where did you get that hat? (*heck*)

Where the heck did you get that hat?

1. I studied but I still flunked the test. (*the devil*)

2. I just deleted three folders on my hard drive. (*darned if*)

3. The police came and scared us. (*the crap*)

4. Christina Aguilera beats Britney Spears any day. (*the heck*)

5. I don't know. (*heck if*)

6. What took you so long? (*the dickens*)

7. Boston pounded Chicago in last night's game. (*the heck*)

8. Didn't she used to go out with Hugo? — Beats me. (*the crap*)

28 To a T

You have already learned all of the most common slang contractions with a verb + *to* that are sometimes shown with slang spellings. The most important ones are:

hafta /ˈhæftə/ = have to

gotta /ˈgɑːtə/ = got to

oughta /ˈɑːtə/ = ought to

sposta /ˈspoʊstə/ = supposed to

wanna /ˈwɑːnə/ = want to

In all of these words except **wanna**, *to* keeps its *t* sound but its *o* sound is shortened to /ə/.

People usually pronounce *to* as /tə/ when speaking informally, even if spelling doesn't show this.

It has to be lunchtime!

Joe wants to go with us

You need to listen more carefully.

I went to the beach yesterday.

Even though the sound is very short, it's important to hear it. You don't have to pronounce *to* in this way; just be sure that you don't miss it when someone else says it.

T and D

Another way in which American spelling and pronunciation are confusing involves *t* and *d*. You already know that many English words ending with *-d* actually have a *t* sound on the end. If the sound before the *-d* is /f/, /k/, /p/, /s/, /θ/, /ʃ/ or /tʃ/, then the *d* is pronounced as a *t*:

crashed /ˈkræʃt/

dissed /ˈdɪst/

rocked /ˈrɑːkt/

popped /ˈpɑːpt/

sleuthed /ˈsluːθt/

surfed /ˈsɚft/

In everyday pronunciaton, -t and -d at the ends of words may be pronounced in exactly the same way if the next sound is a vowel:

"You better *get* going!" /ˈgɛt/
"I just *bought some* new CDs." /ˈbɑːtsəm/
"*Get a* load of this!" /ˈgɛdə/
"I just *bought a* new car." /ˈbɑːdə/
"*What time* are you coming?" /ˌwʌtˈtaɪm/
"I'll *bet* five bucks." /ˈbɛt/
"*What a* stupid thing to do!" /ˈwʌdə/
"I'll *bet a* dollar." /ˈbɛdə/

The slang spellings **whatta** or **whadda** are sometimes used for "what a":

"Whatta great guy he is!"

If the word after a -t is a form of the verb *do,* the t sound often disappears. However, this doesn't happen when the –t word is *that:*

"*What did* he say?" /ˈwʌːdəd/
"I *didn't do* a thing." /ˈdɪdn̩du/
"*What do you* want?" /ˈwʌːdəjə/
"*That didn't* happen." /ˈðætdɪdn̩/

Many questions begin with "What do you." The spelling **Whaddaya** or **Whaddya** is sometimes used to show how it's pronounced (/ˈwʌːdəjə/). For example, you can make a suggestion about something you would like to do by saying "What do you say . . ." before a present-tense sentence:

"Whaddaya say we go have a drink?"

And you can indicate that you don't understand or don't believe something by beginning a question with "What do you mean . . .":

"Whaddaya mean somebody stole my iPod?"

Try It!

In the following sentences (written with standard English spelling), think about the pronunciation. Underline all the letters (and entire words) that would be pronounced as /ə/ in slang. Draw a circle around the *t*'s and the *d*'s that are pronounced the same in conversation. Then say the sentences aloud, using the everyday pronunciation.

1. What do you want, a medal?

2. What about a movie, then a little walk?

3. You should have done better than that.

4. I could have told you what a mistake that was.

5. Did you give them what they wanted?

6. I heard you might have been trying to call me.

7. Why did you say she was going to meet him?

8. Those have to be the hottest babes around.

9. What do you say we get a bite to eat here?

29 A Lowlife Gets Nabbed

Many slang words were originally used by only a few people—criminals or the police, for instance—but slowly became understood by more people, until everyone knew them. Read this conversation between a newspaper editor and a reporter, in which many of the slang words are related to crime.

REPORTER: The cops have nailed a big-time coke dealer.

EDITOR: How'd they get him?

REPORTER: It was a sting. The guy's allegedly in tight with a Bolivian drug kingpin.

EDITOR: Says who?

REPORTER: A San Diego cop who was in on the investigation.

EDITOR: Who did the dirty work?

REPORTER: A rat. A small-time fence who turned rat big-time on some dopers he knew.

EDITOR: What kind of rap sheet does the rat have?

REPORTER: This dude's got a rap sheet as long as a cheap roll of toilet paper. His favorite scam is selling cars he doesn't own. Things haven't gone too well for him since he tried to scam a couple of Feds in Texas.

EDITOR: Will the case hold up?

REPORTER: Hard to say. A good lawyer could beat the rap. The fink is like all these guys: every time his mouth moves he's lying.

EDITOR: Has he done any time for other stuff?

REPORTER: He was sent up on a larceny beef two years ago after copping a plea.

big-time *adjective* important; major

big-time *adverb* in a very obvious way; to an extreme degree

beef *noun* a criminal charge

coke *noun* the drug cocaine

cop *noun* a policeman; **the cops** means "the police"

doper /'doʊpɚ/ *noun* a drug dealer

Fed *noun* a Federal agent, such as an FBI agent

fence *noun* someone who sells stolen goods

fink *noun* a police informer; same as **rat**

kingpin /'kɪŋ,pɪn/ *noun* the boss of an organization, especially an illegal one

lowlife /'loʊ,laɪf/ *noun* a person with no morals

rap sheet *noun* a record of previous arrests

rat *noun* a police informer; same as **fink**

scam *noun* an illegal trick to take someone's money; a fraud

scam *verb* deceive someone to get their money

sting *noun* a scheme for catching criminals by deceiving them

nab *verb* arrest and charge someone with a crime; same as **nail**

nail *verb* arrest and charge someone with a crime; same as **nab**

send sb ⇄ up *phrasal verb* send someone to prison

beat the rap avoid punishment for a criminal charge

cop a plea /'kɑːpə'pliː/ plead guilty to a small crime in order to avoid a trial for a bigger crime

do the dirty work *or* **do sb's dirty work** do something difficult or dangerous for someone else's benefit

do time spend time in prison

in tight with sb in a good or profitable relationship with someone

Says who? /'sɛz'huː/ Who said that? According to whom?

turn rat become a police informer

I. Rewrite the following sentences by substituting slang vocabulary for the underlined words.

EXAMPLE: <u>The police</u> have uncovered a <u>major fraud</u> involving a <u>large number of drug dealers</u>.

The cops have uncovered a big-time scam involving a bunch of dopers.

1. She <u>spent time in prison</u> on a money-laundering <u>charge</u>.

_____

2. He <u>became a police informer</u> in order to <u>avoid punishment on a cocaine charge</u>.

_____

3. The <u>police arrested</u> him for taking a 500-<u>dollar</u> bribe from a <u>federal agent</u>.

_____

4. Why would I want to <u>get into a good relationship</u> with a <u>seller of stolen jewelry</u>?

_____

5. They <u>deceived me</u> into giving them 200 <u>dollars</u>.

_____

II. Make up answers to these questions, using the words in parentheses.

EXAMPLE: Why did he go to prison? (*send up/scam*)

He got sent up for a scam involving stolen cars.

1. Why was his bail set so high? (*kingpin/rap sheet*)

_____

2. Why wouldn't she cooperate? (*the cops/screw over*)

_____

3. How did he avoid prison? (*nail/sting/beat the rap*)

_____

4. What was she nailed for? (*scam/wads/condos*)

_____

5. Who finked on the doper they sent up? (*lowlife/do time/beef*)

_____

Get Yer Stuff 'n' Go

As you know, the pronouns *him, her, it,* and *them* are often contracted in pronunciation. Slang spelling sometimes shows this ("grab 'em").

In slang speech, *your* and *our* sometimes aren't pronounced as you would expect. *Your* and *you're* both have the same pronunciation (/ˈjoɚ/ or /jɚ/) in standard American English, and both may have the same slang spelling: **yer**. So when you hear or read either word, you may have to think about how it's used to know which word is meant.

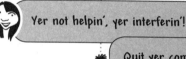

Yer not helpin', yer interferin'!

Quit yer complainin' and do what I tell ya.

"Yer not helpin', yer interferin'!" = You're not helping, you're interfering!
"Quit yer complainin'!" = Quit your complaining!

Another confusing adjective is *our*. The formal pronunciation is /ˈawɚ/, but most Americans often pronounce it /ˈaɚ/. Thus, both *are* and *our* are often pronounced just like the letter *r*.

When *are* isn't stressed, its pronunciation is even shorter: /ɚ/. You have seen this in contractions such as *we're, they're,* and *you're*. In slang spelling, this contraction may occur at the end of question words:

"*What're* you talkin' about?" (= What are) /ˈwʌtɚ/
"*How're* you gonna explain that?" (= How are) /ˈhawɚ/
"*When're* you getting married?" (= When are) /ˈwɛnɚ/
"*Why're* you lookin' at me like that?" (= Why are) /ˈwajɚ/
"*Where're* you from?" (= Where are) /ˈwerɚ/

And remember that auxiliary verbs such as *are* are sometimes left out altogether in slang speech. That is, *are* may be contracted so much that there's nothing left of it!

When are you getting married?

When're you gettin' married?

When ya gettin' married?

'n' That's Not All

The word *and* also gets very short pronunciation in informal speech. The pronunciation is /ən/, and it's often shown in slang spelling by **'n'**:

"Bob 'n' Kathy're comin' with us."

"Sun 'n' fun is all I'm looking for on vacation."

"Yer sister 'n' my brother used to go out."

Try It!

Read the following sentences out loud, paying close attention to the pronunciation of the underlined words. In the blank after each sentence, write the standard English equivalent of the underlined words.

EXAMPLE: When're ya gonna gimme my money? _____*When are you going to give me*_____

1. Whadda buncha suckers ya'll are!

   _____

2. Yer gonna hafta lemme take 'em.

   _____

3. When've we gotta return our stuff 'n' be outta here?

   _____

4. Whatcha say we give 'im loadsa trouble?

   _____

5. I betcha ten bucks he got yer spot.

   _____

6. Ya shoulda dropped yer classes 'n' got yerself a better job.

   _____

7. That woulda set ya back big-time! _____

8. Didja think I mighta forgotten 'n' left ya here?

   _____

9. Why'd ya say they're outta tickets?

   _____

10. Put yer money where yer mouth is.

    _____

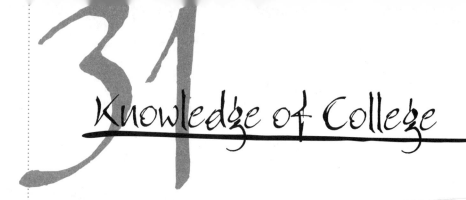

Knowledge of College

Some slang is called "college slang" because it's mainly used by students in colleges and universities. But you don't have to be a student to use it. Follow the story of Stuart, Eli, and Jeff to learn some words that are totally cool!

for real *adjective and adverb* sincere; telling the truth

hip *adjective* cool

babe *noun* an attractive young women (used mostly by men; sometimes offensive to women)

bone up (on sth) *phrasal verb* learn about something by studying it

cram *verb* study hard before an exam

kick, kick it *verb* relax; chill

no stress don't worry; don't get upset

clueless *adjective* ignorant; not informed about something

old-skool, old-school *adjective* old-fashioned; not current or popular

booty call *noun* a telephone call, meeting, or person that is only for sex

hoochie *noun* a sexy young woman (may be offensive to women)

number *noun* a woman, especially when considered for her attractiveness

dog *verb* tease

pick sb ⇄ up *phrasal verb* introduce yourself to someone and have sex

school *verb* give someone lessons or instructions about something

score *verb* succeed in having sex with someone you meet

Action stations! Do something! (used to show that some action is required)

give sb/sth the green light give someone permission to do something

lose your edge lose an advantage or skill that you have had

digits *noun* someone's phone number. If you **bust sb's digits**, you get their telephone number.

jack sth ⇌ up *phrasal verb* mess something up; ruin something

pass on sb/sth *phrasal verb* decide you don't want to do something or get involved with someone

Can you dig it? Do you understand? (sometimes used to show surprise or pleasure at what has happened)

What's the deal? What's happening? (used to say that you don't quite understand what is happening or has happened)

Try It!

Read the three comic strips again and study the vocabulary. Then decide whether these statements are true (T) or false (F), and circle your answer.

1. Jeff succeeds in picking up a girl in the bar.	T	F
2. Jeff must study for an exam tonight.	T	F
3. The new campus bar isn't very popular.	T	F
4. Stuart and Eli think Taylor is attractive.	T	F
5. The girl in the bar is mainly attracted to Stuart.	T	F
6. The bar plays music that's very popular now.	T	F
7. Taylor gave Jeff her telephone number.	T	F
8. Jeff memorizes Taylor's number before giving it to Eli.	T	F

Whaddaya Think?

In Unit 3 you learned several one-word responses:

Yay!

Bummer!

Duh!

Wild!

Gosh!

Many other slang words are used to show that you think something is either very good or very bad:

How's the new James Bond movie?

It rocks.

It sucks.

rock *verb* be very good, superior, or pleasant

suck *verb* be very bad, inferior, or unpleasant

Here are some adjectives for saying you like something a lot:

awesome very good and impressive: "The special effects in that movie are awesome."

da bomb *(predicate)* the best; very cool: "The costumes are da bomb."

incredible surprisingly good: "The acting is really incredible."

great very good: "The ending is great!"

monster big and impressive: "There's a monster chase scene in it."

Here are some adjectives for saying you don't like something:

lame, lamo /'leɪmoʊ/ inferior; completely inadequate: "All the shoot-'em-up scenes are lame."

the pits (*predicate*) very bad: "The acting is really the pits."

sucky very bad: "The soundtrack is pretty sucky."

tacky showing bad taste: "The love scenes were really tacky."

wack, whack bad; inferior; crazy: "The plot is totally wack."

People usually spend more time criticizing than praising, so there seem to be many more slang ways for saying that something is bad:

The cheesy dialogue was inexcusable. And the sound effects were really half-assed.

Yeah, I can't believe Spielberg would put his name on such a turkey. What a letdown.

Are you guys still trashing that movie? How dare you dis my favorite director's work!

cheesy /'tʃi:zi/ *adjective* annoying and bad because of bad taste

half-assed /'hæf'æst/ *adjective* inferior; poorly done (may be offensive)

letdown /'lɛt,daʊn/ *noun* a disappointing thing or experience

turkey *noun* a very inferior product or experience

trash *verb* say bad things about someone or something

dis /'dɪs/ *verb* show disrespect for someone or something

I. Fill in the blanks with one of the words from this unit's vocabulary. Some sentences require a positive word and some a negative word.

EXAMPLE: The flight was basically OK but the food was really _____*sucky*_____.

1. Except for the lousy sound system, the party really _____.

2. Two of the singers were sick so the concert was a real _____.

3. The food at the reception was _____, and that kinda made up for the boring speeches.

4. All of the reviews _____ the acting, but I didn't think the movie was that bad.

5. Our hotel room was a little noisy, but the view from the window was _____!

6. She's got a hot body, but you don't notice it because of the _____ clothes she wears.

7. She told a totally _____ joke and nobody laughed except her.

II. Write It!

1. Think about a movie, concert, party, vacation, or other experience that you really enjoyed. Write a short paragraph about it, using these words: *great, awesome, incredible, rock (verb)*.

_____

_____

_____

_____

_____

_____

_____

2. Think about a movie, concert, party, vacation, or other experience that you didn't enjoy at all. Write a short paragraph about it, using these words: *letdown, lame, the pits, turkey*.

_____

_____

_____

_____

_____

_____

_____

Friggin' Intense

In Unit 27 you saw some expressions that people use to add emphasis, including words like **darned** and **damned**. Forms of these words are used in other ways to show what you think about something, usually when you don't like it.

The dang thing won't start.

It ate the whole darned pizza!

These damn mosquitoes are driving me crazy!

Turn down that friggin' music!

Darned, **damned**, and **danged** are often used before a noun to show that the thing you are talking about is annoying you. Because people don't pronounce these words carefully, the *-ed* is sometimes dropped: **darn, damn, dang**. Some people think **damn** is offensive; most people think **goddamn** (which is used the same way) is offensive.

Frigging (friggin'), **fricking (frickin')**, **freaking (freakin')**, and **flaming (flamin')** are also used before nouns, often to show that you're annoyed. These words are all substitutes for **fucking**, which is used in the same way but is rude and offensive.

As you see, all of these words can also modify adjectives. The adjective may be either negative or positive; the modifying word simply makes it stronger.

    friggin' hot = very hot

    damn lucky = extremely lucky

An adverb that makes the meaning of an adjective more or less intense is sometimes called an *intensive*. Here are some standard English intensives, arranged from weak to strong:

    slightly → somewhat → rather → quite → very → extremely → completely

In slang and informal speech, people may use a different set of intensives:

    a little, a bit → kind of, sort of → pretty → way → really → totally

(Remember that **kind of** and **sort of** often have the slang spellings **kinda** and **sorta**.)

The intensives *pretty*, *so*, and *too* are often used before **darn**, **damn**, and the intensives that start with *f-*. This use is only for emphasis:

"If yer so damned smart, why ain't ya rich?"

"I make a pretty darn good lasagna."

"I'm too freakin' busy to think about that now."

Another slang intensive is **as all get-out** /æz,ɑːlˈgɛt,aʊt/, which is used after an adjective. It means "very" or "extremely":

"The music was great but the plot was stupid as all get-out."

"The posters totally suck. I mean, they're ugly as all get-out."

Try It!

Rewrite the sentences below, inserting the words in parentheses.

EXAMPLE: I forgot about the board meeting. (*darn, totally*)

I totally forgot about the darn board meeting.

1. Isn't it early to start your moaning? (*friggin', a little*)

_____

2. It was so cold that the pipes froze. (*freakin', damn*)

_____

3. That's a lame excuse. (*frickin'*)

_____

4. Life's too short to put up with such nonsense. (*freakin'*)

_____

5. This may be stupid, but what did he actually mean? (*way*)

_____

6. The food was disappointing, but the show was cool. (*totally, kinda*)

_____

Alien Objects Approaching

In Unit D you saw a phrase from Spanish (**Qué pasa?**) that is used informally in English as a greeting. Now let's have a look at some other foreign words and phrases that have entered English as slang. The definitions below give the *English* meaning of the words, which may be different from the meaning in the original language.

When Americans want to sound refined, often in a humorous way, they enjoy using French.

au contraire /ˌoʊkɑnˈtreɚ/ on the contrary; just the opposite (of what someone else has said): "Au contraire—I really do like him."

beaucoup /ˈboʊku/ **1.** *adjective* many; a lot of: "You can bet somebody is making beaucoup bucks off of that scam." **2.** *adverb* much; a lot: "I finally realized that I missed him beaucoup." **3.** *noun* a lot: "I've invested beaucoup in my education and I can't walk away from it now."

moi /ˈmwɑ:/ *pronoun* **1.** me: "Don't count on moi forking over 20 bucks for that." **2.** my: "We took a cab to moi house."

quelle /ˈkɛl/ *adjective and adverb* a lot; big; very: "Quelle surprise—I didn't win the lottery this week."

tres /ˈtreɪ/ *adverb* very: "The movie was tres funny and really kooky."

Yiddish is a language similar to German that used to be spoken by many Jews in Europe. When European Jews emigrated to the U.S. in the 19th and 20th centuries, they brought a lot of slang with them!

dreck *noun* crap: "How can you watch that dreck on TV night after night?"

kvetch /ˈkvɛtʃ/ *verb* complain constantly: "At the restaurant they spent the whole time kvetching about the bad service."

schlep /ˈʃlɛp/ *verb* go somewhere or carry something with difficulty: "Get a babysitter—I'm not schlepping that brat all over town with me."

schlock /ˈʃlɑːk/ *noun* junk; crap: "All they had to eat was some old doughnuts and other schlock."

schmuck /ˈʃmʌk/ *noun* **1.** an annoying person who you don't like: "Some schmuck hit my car in the parking lot." **2.** an ordinary person: "Look at all those poor schmucks waiting to get through customs."

There are many Spanish-speakers in the U.S., and some of them speak "Spanglish"—a language that mixes Spanish and English. We have already seen **nada** (= zero, nothing), which is a Spanish word. The following Spanish words are also often used in American slang:

cojones /kəˈhoʊneɪz/ *noun* courage: "Congress didn't have the cojones to stand up to that cowboy president."

dineros /dɪˈneroʊz/ *noun* dollars; money: "It costs a few dineros more, but it's worth it."

mañana /mɑnˈjɑːnə/ *adverb* tomorrow: "I'm going mañana to have my tongue pierced."

mucho /ˈmuːtʃoʊ/ *adverb* much; a lot; very: "A bunch of stupid stuff happened and I was mucho annoyed."

Because Italian is closely related to Spanish, it's hard to say which language some words came from. **Numero uno**, for example, means "number one" in both languages. In American slang it means "the best." Here are some other words from Italian:

bimbo /'bɪmboʊ/ *noun* an attractive but stupid person: "The bimbo at the checkout couldn't even count change right."

ciao /'tʃaʊ/ hello; good-bye

mondo /'mɑːndoʊ/ *adverb* very: "There was mondo crazy traffic on the way home."

primo /'priːmoʊ/ *adjective* very good; the best: "We both got massages, then we ate some primo chocolate."

Try It!

I. Find a word from this unit that will complete the sentences below. Use plurals if you need to.

1. No one has the _____ to tell them they screwed up.

2. If all you're going to do is _____, why don't you just leave?

3. It's got a flashy video, but the song itself is just _____.

4. You're gonna be in _____ trouble when your dad sees this.

5. He always dates blonde _____ and then wonders why he's bored.

6. We met up with _____ cousin and had a beer.

7. I'd like to go but I haven't got the _____ just now.

8. We just got a _____ scanner that makes perfect copies.

9. Don't look now, but some _____ just took your parking place.

10. Tina scored _____ points for handing her paper in early.

II. Here are some words from other languages—Japanese, Dutch, and Russian—that are used in American slang. For each one, use a dictionary to find out its meaning.

1. honcho   2. cop *(verb)*   3. nyet

What's the Buzz?

Slang is mostly talk. Talk is mostly about getting and giving information. The slang terms above all refer to information.

the dope/the lowdown/the skinny = reliable information that explains something

inside line information that only a few people have, especially information that gives them an advantage: "He's got an inside line on jobs because his dad works at the company."

the buzz what people are saying about something: "I decided to skip the *Spider-Man* sequel after hearing the buzz about it."

I don't like parties 'cause I'm no good at schmoozing.

I'd rather rap with one of my peeps any day—seems like I can yammer on for hours doin' that.

But I hate it when folks start dishin' the dirt on others and shootin' off their mouths about who's doin' what to who.

And if they ask me for the goods on somebody I keep my mouth shut so they won't go blabbin' it somewhere else.

Many other slang words are about different kinds of talking:

the goods *noun* information about someone, especially if it's damaging

blab *verb* talk about or say something that should be secret

rap *verb* talk; have a conversation

schmooze *verb* talk with people informally, especially to persuade them or get something from them

yammer *verb* talk, talk too much

dish the dirt talk about other people's personal lives; gossip

shoot your mouth ⇄ off talk about something that should be secret

DID YOU KNOW?

Rap has many slang meanings, some related to talk and some related to crime. You learned **rap sheet** (= record of arrests), and **beat the rap** (= avoid punishment) in Unit 29. A person who **takes the rap** gets blamed for something bad that happened.

A person who **gets a bad rap** has a bad reputation: "His band is getting a bad rap because they don't show up for their gigs."

A **bum rap** is a bad reputation that isn't deserved: "I think she got a bum rap for doing something anyone would have done."

Someone's **rap** is what they have to say, especially if they're trying to persuade you: "I listened to his rap but it didn't convince me." Someone's **rap** can also mean the rap music that they perform.

When people sit around talking about nothing in particular, you can say they are **shooting the breeze/bull/gift** or **shooting the shit** (offensive): "We spent the whole evening just shootin' the breeze."

When you talk seriously about a subject in a direct way, you can say that you're **talking turkey**: "It's time to talk turkey with your boss and find out how much you're worth to him."

Try It!

Use the term in parentheses to make up answers to these questions.

EXAMPLE: Why did the cops let her go? (*the goods*)

They didn't really have the goods on her.

1. Why did the cops let her go? (take the rap)

   _____

2. Why did the cops let her go? (*beat the rap*)

   _____

3. Why did the cops let her go? (*the lowdown*)

   _____

4. Where can I find out who did this? (*the skinny*)

   _____

5. Where can I find out who did this? (*the buzz*)

   _____

6. How did you find that out? (*dish the dirt*)

   _____

7. How did you find that out? (*blab*)

   _____

8. How did you find that out? (*shoot the breeze*)

   _____

9. What reason did he give for losing his job? (*bad rap*)

   _____

10. What reason did he give for losing his job? (*bum rap*)

   _____

Cheap Substitutes

Often the only difference between informal and standard English is a choice of words. This is especially true with verbs. For example, the verb *return* has many alternatives in informal conversation. Instead of using it, people use many different phrasal verbs. *Return* could be used in any of the following sentences:

"What time will you come back?"
"Let's get back to the main topic."
"Give it back to her right now."
"I have to go back tonight."
"Did you take back the DVDs?"
"Turn it back to the low setting."

When people speak or write informally, it's very common to use phrasal verbs instead of standard English verbs. Let's check out a few of them:

bag on = complain (about)

get sb down = depress

butt in = interrupt

clam up = become silent; stop talking

goof up = bungle; make a mess of

He got kicked out for swearing at the zebra.

kick out = expel

Does that really turn you on?

turn sb on = stimulate, especially sexually

I really wiped out on that last curve.

wipe out = crash

Wow! They ripped off the whole ATM machine.

rip sth ⇄ off = steal

More Substitutions

Another way that people make ordinary language more slangy is to use different prepositions after a verb. Sometimes the result will look like a phrasal verb, when it is really just a verb followed by a prepositional phrase. The most common substitution is to use *off of* or *off* instead of *from* in verbs about taking or receiving:

Listen to this song I just bought off iTunes.

That's a bad habit he learned off his father.

They probably stole it off the back of a truck.

Here are some other examples:

"I found it off a link from a blog I read all the time."

"He says he got it off of a Web site."

"I taped *Lord of the Rings* off of pay-per-view at my parents."

Try It!

Choose a word from Group A and one from Group B to complete the sentences below. The phrasal verb you create should have the meaning of the word or words in parentheses. You will probably need to use a dictionary.

GROUP A	GROUP B
break, hit, kiss, knock, make, play, sell, throw, wear	around, back, down, off, on, out, up

EXAMPLE: I heard that Tanya and Jason _____*broke*_____ _*up*_. (*end a relationship*)

1. She can _____ _____ three martinis and still act normal. (*drink*)

2. I'm going to _____ _____ a few ideas to get the conversation started. (*introduce*)

3. I think somebody has _____ _____ with my pen. (*steal*)

4. He's _____ _____ to the boss 'cause he wants Friday off. (*act nice to get what you want from someone*)

5. In that outfit the guys will start _____ _____ you as soon as you walk in. (*show sexual interest*)

6. He _____ _____ all of his old clients and now he wants them back. (*dismiss*)

7. He _____ her _____ and now he wants her to get an abortion. (*make pregnant*)

8. When she got hip to the fact that she might get canned, she decided it would be easier to _____ us all _____. (*betray*)

9. He's working on a Ph.D. at Princeton, but he always tries to _____ that _____. (*give little importance to; minimize*).

Is It Love?

Remember Eli and Jeff's cousin Taylor? They've been going out together.

> Eli and Taylor really hit it off from the get-go. Usually she doesn't like guys macking on her, but this time she took the bait.

> Before you know it they were making out like crazy.

> It was embarrassing watching my cousin suck face in public. Now whenever you see them they're all over each other.

> I think Eli just does it so other guys won't hit on her. Not like he has to worry.

> Yeah, everyone knows they're an item.

> And nobody's going to put the moves on her when he's got her in a lip-lock!

an item *noun* two people who are sexually or romantically involved

lip-lock /'lɪp,lɑːk/ *noun* a long kiss

hit on sb show sexual interest in someone by talking to them; similar to **mack on**

go out *phrasal verb* **1.** go on a date **2.** (**be going out**) be romantically involved with someone

mack on sb *phrasal verb* show sexual interest in someone by talking to them; similar to **hit on sb**. Another way of saying this is **lay the mack on sb**.

make out *phrasal verb* hug and kiss

be all over sb touch someone in a romantic or sexual way

from the get-go from the very beginning

hit it off (with sb) get along very well

like crazy a lot

put the moves on sb show your sexual interest to someone

suck face kiss

take the bait accept something offered to you

Love and sexual relationships are a very popular subject among friends, and most of the words that young people use to talk about them are slang. There are many different ways of saying that one person is attracted to another:

"Taylor has a huge **crush** on Eli."
"Taylor is **crushing on** Eli in a big way."
"Taylor really **has a thing for** Eli."
"Eli has got **the hots** for Taylor."
"Eli is **wild about** Taylor."
"Eli thinks Taylor is totally **hot**."

But love doesn't last forever. So some slang words and expressions are about what happens when a relationship ends.

Looks like Eli and Taylor are splitsville. I heard he kicked her to the curb.

Au contraire, dude. Taylor dumped him when she found out he was seein' that chick there, Ramona.

Doesn't look like she wasted any time finding a new squeeze.

Yeah, he's the same guy that Ramona gave the kiss-off to when she met Eli!

chick *noun* a young woman, especially an attractive one. (Some women find this word offensive.)

kiss-off *noun* a message to someone that you are finished with them

splitsville *noun or adjective* the end of a relationship; broken up

squeeze *noun* a boyfriend or girlfriend

dump sb *verb* end a relationship with someone

kick/take sb to the curb get rid of someone

Try It!

I. Answer these questions based on your own experience (or make up answers if you prefer), using the words or expressions in parentheses.

1. Have you ever sucked face in public? (*lip-lock*)

_____

2. When is the last time someone hit on you? (*put the moves on*)

_____

3. Did you ever give the kiss-off to a boyfriend or girlfriend? (*dump*)

_____

4. Is it true that you've got a new squeeze? (*item*)

_____

5. Is there anybody you've been crushing on? (*the hots*)

_____

6. Why do guys always think they've got to impress girls? (*lay the mack, chicks*)

_____

II. Write a story, two or three paragraphs long, about a relationship that you had and that ended. Use the vocabulary from this lesson and earlier lessons. Make sure that it answers the following questions.

1. How did you meet?   2. What were your feelings about this person at first?
3. How long did the relationship last?   4. What happened to change it?   5. How did it end?

_____
_____
_____
_____
_____
_____
_____
_____
_____
_____
_____
_____

38

If the Shoe Fits . . .

You made a big deal out of wanting to see her, then you blew off your date, and now you don't call her back.

When you put it that way, you make me sound like a jerk.

Well, if the shoe fits!

An old expression goes, **If the shoe fits, wear it**. Often people shorten it to "**If the shoe fits**." You usually say it to show that you agree with a description of someone, even though the description is negative.

A **jerk** is someone whose behavior is offensive, and who has no consideration for other people. A stronger (and offensive) word with a similar meaning is **asshole**. People use these words more often about men than about women.

Many other slang words describe qualities of people—usually (but not always) negative ones. Here are some popular slang adjectives:

Adjectives	**cheesy** not fashionable; not showing good taste or understanding of what is popular. Similar words are **dorky, uncool**, and **out of it**	**clueless** not understanding; without any knowledge; stupid. **Dopey** has a similar meaning.	**hot** sexually attractive (both men and women). **Buff** is used more for men alone, and **bootylicious** /ˌbuːtiˈlɪʃəs/ for women, but both words are used for both sexes.
Someone who is always this way	**dweeb** /ˈdwiːb/, **dork** /ˈdoɚk/, **nerd** /ˈnɚd/	**bozo** /ˈboʊzoʊ/, **dipstick**, **dipshit** (offensive), **dope**, **doofus** /ˈduːfəs/, **nitwit**, **pinhead**	**babe** (for a woman), **stud** (for a man), **hottie** (for both)

Adjectives	**klutzy** /ˈklʌtsi/ clumsy	**pissed off** angry (sometimes offensive)	**sleazy** without morals; dishonest
Someone who is always this way	**klutz** /ˈklʌts/, **spaz**	**hothead**	**dirtball, lowlife, scumbag**

Adjectives	**spacey** tending to forget things; unable to focus attention. **Flaky** has a similar meaning.	**stoked** /ˈstoʊkl/ very enthusiastic about something. **Pumped** has a similar meaning.	**huffy** impatient and easily angered
Someone who is always this way	**flake, space cadet**		**bitch** (offensive)

Totally Wack

Wack usually means "crazy" (though it can also mean simply "inferior"). It can describe a person or an action. A special group of words describes behavior or people who are a little bit . . . crazy! However, they're not often used for someone who is actually mentally ill.

All of these adjectives—**nuts, bananas, bonkers, ditzy, wack**—mean "crazy" or "very stupid." **Cracked, loopy,** and **out of your mind** mean the same thing.

Certain nouns mean "a crazy person." They are usually insulting, and people often use them to talk about someone who isn't present.

All these words—**basket case, crackpot, ditz, kook,** and **screwball**—mean a person whose behavior is crazy. Like the adjectives, they don't often mean that a person is mentally ill—just that he or she has done something very strange.

Try It!

I. Fill in the blanks with a noun or adjective from this lesson.

EXAMPLE: I'm not that enthusiastic about the movie, but Joe's totally ___*pumped*___.

1. I get a little _____ sometimes and forget to check the time, but my boyfriend is a total _____.

2. Our _____ mayor got caught taking bribes. He's such a _____.

3. Which _____ _____ thought you could drive the car without brakes?

4. He interrupts anyone who's speaking and says something rude—he's just a total _____.

II. Write two comments in response to each sentence below, using the vocabulary from this unit. One sentence should contain an adjective and the other should contain a noun. Remember that many of these words can hurt people's feelings—be careful about when you use them.

EXAMPLE: George drops the ball every time you throw it to him.

A. ___*Yeah, he's really klutzy.*___   B. ___*I know. He's a spaz.*___

1. She's got such an attitude! Ask her anything and she just shouts "No!"

A. _____   B. _____

2. Did you see that suit John was wearing? That is so last year!

A. _____   B. _____

3. Check out the football player that Kaitlin hooked up with. Wow!

A. _____   B. _____

4. Did she really put M&Ms in the dog's dish?

A. _____   B. _____

5. Did you hear that Lauren got a modeling contract?

A. _____   B. _____

6. Karen got out of her car with the engine running and then locked all the doors. Now she can't get back in!

A. _____   B. _____

39

A Setup Job

Nouns and adjectives are sometimes made from putting the two parts of a phrasal verb together. You may already know some standard English words formed in this way:

back up *(verb)*	backup *(noun, adjective)*
count down *(verb)*	countdown *(noun)*
drop out *(verb)*	dropout *(noun)*
take out *(verb)*	takeout, take-out *(noun, adjective)*

If a phrasal verb is slang, a noun or adjective made from it is usually also slang. Here are some examples from words you have seen earlier:

75 bucks! What a rip-off!

Who's the chick with Jason?

Probably some pickup from the beach.

I had a huge wipeout halfway down the hill!

This is the hangout everybody's been talking about.

hangout *noun* a place where people hang out

pickup *noun* a person who you pick up, especially for sex

rip-off *noun* an instance of someone stealing or charging too much

wipeout *noun* an accident, especially on a bicycle, skis, a skateboard, etc.

Nouns made from phrasal verbs are always stressed on the first syllable. They are usually spelled as one word, but sometimes they have a hyphen, and sometimes it is okay to spell them either way.

Here are some other slang phrasal verbs, along with the nouns related to them:

 Mr. Kosman really blew up at the meeting.

Mr. Kosman had a huge blowup at the meeting

 They really screwed up the job.

The whole job was a screwup.

We really chowed down at my uncle's.

We had a great chowdown at my uncle's.

 Mostly what he does is goof off all the time.

He's just a big goof-off.

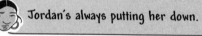 Jordan's always putting her down.

Everything he says about her is a put-down.

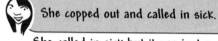 She copped out and called in sick.

She called in sick but it was just a cop-out.

blowup an explosion of anger

chowdown a meal

cop-out a failure to meet your responsibilities

goof-off a person who wastes a lot of time

put-down an insult or disrespectful comment

screwup a big mistake; a person who always makes mistakes

RATED X

Some vulgar words also form slang phrasal verbs and nouns. Men use these words more than women. Most people find them offensive; you shouldn't use them. Two common offensive phrasal verbs that form nouns are:

fuck up bungle (same as **screw up**). A **fuckup** is a person who never does anything right, or a problem that is the result of big mistakes: "It's hard to teach when half the students are such fuckups." "There was another fuckup and now the whole thing will be two days late."

jerk off masturbate. A **jerk-off** is a person who irritates you, especially by being foolish, lazy, or annoying.

Try It!

I. The words underlined in the sentences below are either phrasal verbs or nouns made from phrasal verbs. For each sentence, write a different sentence with the same meaning. Use a noun if the original sentence contains an underlined phrasal verb; use a phrasal verb if the original sentence contains an underlined noun. If you aren't sure of the meaning of some of the words, use a dictionary. (If the dictionary shows only the phrasal verb, you may have to guess the meaning of the noun based on it.)

EXAMPLE: Janelle hooked up with Todd at one of the sports bars.

Janelle and Todd had a hookup at one of the sports bars.

1. We thought the electricity had really gone off but it was a fakeout.

2. We were expected to kick back 10% of the profits to their agent.

3. The government has bailed out the company for the third time.

4. Somebody's been getting a huge rake-off from the casino's profits.

5. Doug finally sold out and got a job as a corporate lawyer.

6. He's really cute, but his bad breath is a huge turn-off.

II. Answer these questions, using the phrasal verb that the underlined word comes from.

1. What is a blowoff class? _____

2. How do you know when someone is suffering from burnout?

3. What sort of meal would you describe as a pig-out?

4. What kind of a movie would you describe as a gross-out?

It Feels Nice to Say It Twice!

All languages have words or phrases in which the second part is the same as the first or sounds like the first. English has many that you may already know, including *bigwig, chitchat, humdrum, knickknack, payday, seesaw,* and *zigzag*.

Many such words and phrases are slang. Let's sneak a peak at a few of them!

okeydokey /ˌoʊkiˈdoʊki/ *adverb* yes (a form of OK)

jeez Louise /ˌdʒiːzləˈwiːz/ *interjection* used to express surprise

boob tube *noun* television

creature feature *noun* a scary film, especially one with monsters

doo-doo *noun* human or animal waste; poop

fag hag *noun* a woman who likes gay men

fender bender *noun* a minor accident in a car

boy toy *noun* an attractive young man

same ol' same ol' the same thing: used to say that nothing has changed, or that something is the same as before

sneak a peek have a look. A **sneak peek** is a look at something before others have been allowed to look.

Who knew? used to express surprise at what someone has said

Sometimes people use a rhyming word after a phrase just because it rhymes.

See you later, alligator.

After a while, crocodile.

What's the plan, Stan?

Cut me some slack, Jack!

cut sb some slack be patient with someone

Try It!

I. Match each word in column A to its definition in column B, and write the correct letters in the blanks below.

1. **chick flick** ____
2. **fake bake** ____
3. **fat cat** ____
4. **flip-flop** ____
5. **hotshot** ____
6. **itsy-bitsy, teensy-weensy** __
7. **lovey-dovey** ____
8. **no-show** ____
9. **palsy-walsy** ____
10. **slo-mo** ____

A. a movie that women like
B. a sudden change of opinion or position
C. a tan produced by rubbing brown liquid on the skin
D. an important or influential person
E. extremely small
F. very affectionate
G. film speed that is slower than normal
H. someone expected who doesn't arrive
I. someone who thinks he or she is very impressive
J. very friendly, or pretending to be very friendly

II. Fill in the blanks, using a word from the list above or one from the vocabulary in this unit. You will need to use a plural in some cases. Be sure to read your completed sentences out loud.

1. This lawyer thinks he's a real _____, but the judge wasn't very impressed.

2. I've been driving in _____ for the last two hours because of a _____ on the freeway.

3. This theater's only showing a _____ and a _____.

4. She was totally ticked off with me yesterday, but now she's done a _____ and she's all _____.

5. The best seats in the front are reserved for some _____, but if there are any _____ you can have their seats.

6. She's got this little _____ _____ in her kitchen—the screen is only six inches wide.

Don't Try This at Home

In Units 27 and 33 you learned some words and expressions that people use to emphasize what they're saying. Some of these words, and others, are used in other ways to express different feelings and attitudes.

For chrissake! Watch where the hell you're going!

Damn it! I smashed my thumb!

Holy moly! We better go inside!

All of these expressions (**Damn it!, For chrissake!, Holy moly!**) are sometimes called *oaths*. Some oaths are offensive and others are not. Let's look at how these words differ, and what they add to a sentence.

"Accident" oaths: People use certain expressions when something bad happens by chance. Oaths like these are similar to **gosh** and other words that you learned in Unit 3. Often people use a mild oath (not offensive) when they're a little upset, and a strong oath (offensive) when they're very upset.

Darn!, Darn it! (very mild, sometimes humorous)

Damn!, Damn it! (sometimes offensive)

Goddamn!, Goddammit! /ˈgɑːdˈdæmɪt/ (usually offensive)

"Annoyance" oaths: People may use these when they're mildly irritated at something that someone else has done:

> **Criminy!** /ˈkrɪməni/
>
> **Jeez!, Geez!** /ˈdʒiːz/

"Angry" oaths: People use these when they're mad:

> **Damn!, Damn it!** (sometimes offensive)
>
> **For chrissake!** /fəˈkraɪsˈseɪk/
> ("For Christ's sake"—sometimes offensive)
>
> **Christ Almighty!, Jesus Christ!** (sometimes offensive)
>
> **Goddamn!, Goddammit!** (usually offensive)

Even stronger than **Goddamn!** are **Shit!** and **Fuck!**, which some people use when they're genuinely angry or upset. **For fuck's sake!** and **For shit's sake!** are just as strong. You may hear these expressions, but don't use them!

"Surprise" oaths: People use these when something unexpected happens, or to show irritation in a not very serious way:

> **Gee whiz!** (mild, sometimes humorous)
>
> **Holy moly!, Holy Toledo!** (mild, sometimes humorous)
>
> **Holy shit!** (sometimes offensive)

What the f***!

What the heck/hell/fuck! These expressions are used to show that you don't understand what's happening or that you're very upset about it. **What the heck!** is very mild. Some people think **What the hell!** is offensive. But most people are offended by **What the fuck!**—you shouldn't use it.

But sometimes these same expressions just mean "Okay" or "Why not?" It all depends on the tone of the speaker's voice.

Holy moly! We better go inside!

Sure, what the heck! It beats getting wet.

Try It!

Review the units that have discussed one-word reactions (Unit 3), expressions that show agreement or disagreement (Unit 17), emphasis words (Units 27 and 33), and negative words (Unit 33). Then write a possible response to each of the following sentences or questions:

EXAMPLE: What did you think of the president's speech last night?

I thought it was a crock.

1. Why didn't they leave any food for us? They knew we were coming back.

2. I decided I'd just give you some money for your birthday.

3. I think I just deleted all the files you were working on.

4. Boy, women sure know how to make you feel guilty for being late.

5. Why can't I turn it up a little louder? I can hardly hear it.

6. Do you think it's OK to just ignore these parking tickets?

42 Time for Some Answers

You have learned words that people use to show their reactions (Unit 3), to show that they agree or disagree (Unit 17), and to express surprise or anger (Unit 42). But sometimes all you want to say is "Yes" or "No"!

Anybody wanna check out the new bowling alley with me?

Nah

Yeah

Uh-huh

Yup

Not in this lifetime

Nope

No way

Sure

You bet

Yuppers

Not a chance

Uh-uh

A question that begins with a verb, or with the helping verb left out (as in the "Anybody wanna . . . " sentence above, which would normally start with "Does"), usually only requires an answer of "Yes" or "No." There are many slang and informal ways to say yes and no.

Yes	*No*
Sure	**Uh-uh**
Uh-huh	**Nah** /ˈnæ/ or /ˈnɑː/
Yeah /ˈjɛə/	**No way**
You bet, You betcha	**Nope**
Yup /ˈjʌp/	**Not a chance**
Yuppers /ˈjʌpɚz/	**Not in this lifetime**

IT MAKES A DIFFERENCE

Look at these two words and their pronunciations:

  uh-huh /ˌʌˈhʌ/   **uh-uh** /ˈʌˌʌ/

Uh-huh means "yes." The second syllable is always pronounced at a higher pitch than the first.

Uh-uh means "no." The second syllable is always pronounced at a lower pitch than the first.

To show that you didn't hear (or didn't understand) what someone has said to you, you may say "Pardon me?" "Excuse me?" or "What did you say?" But in informal speech, you have a few more choices:

Come again? is a way of asking someone to repeat what they just said. **Say what?** is a slangier way of doing it.

How's that? or **What's that?** means that you didn't hear or understand. They are usually pronounced /ˈhaʊˌzæt/ and /ˈwʌtsˌæt/; sometimes you will see a slang spelling such as **Howzat?** or **Whats'at?** or **Whazzat?**

Huh? usually means "I didn't hear you." But sometimes it shows that you're surprised, you're confused, you don't believe what someone has said, or you think that what someone has said isn't appropriate.

Often people respond to a question or to new information with a question of their own. Sometimes the question is simply a way of expressing an idea:

How'd you guess? /ˈhaʊdʒəˈgɛs/ (= How did you guess?) means "Yes." But people only say it when the answer is obvious, so it's usually sarcastic.

Who wants to know? People say this only if they think that you don't have a good reason for asking your question, and that you may be trying to get information for someone else.

Try It!

Write three responses to each sentence below, responding in the way indicated in parentheses.

EXAMPLE: Got 20 bucks you can lend me?

a. (no) _____*Nah, I'm all tapped out.*_____

b. (yes) _____*Sure, when do I get it back?*_____

c. (anger) _____*Geez! Why don't you get a job?*_____

1. You gonna stop for gas pretty soon?

a. (no) _____

b. (yes) _____

c. (surprise) _____

2. They just said your name over the intercom.

a. (surprise) _____

b. (anger) _____

c. (enthusiasm) _____

3. Looks like somebody drove into the back of your car.

a. (accident) _____

b. (anger) _____

c. (disappointment) _____

4. Did you pass the English test?

a. (yes) _____

b. (no) _____

c. (suspicion) _____

43 Win Some, Lose Some

blow sb ⇄ away *phrasal verb* defeat someone

tank *verb* fail completely

bring the heat increase your efforts

kick some butt show that you're powerful and superior. If you **kick somebody's butt**, you defeat them. Something that **kicks butt** is very powerful and impressive: "It's a small car but it really kicks butt." All these expressions can also be used with **ass** instead of **butt**, but many people find **ass** offensive.

Ouch! *exclamation* used to express sudden mental pain (in standard English it expresses physical pain)

In the story above, all the following slang verbs mean "defeat," though most of them have other meanings as well: **clobber, cream, slaughter, smear, stomp, whomp, whup.**

All these verbs behave in the same way in sentences: (1) They're all transitive: "We clobbered/stomped/whupped 'em." (2) They're all often used passively, with *get:* "The Pistons really got creamed/smeared/whomped last night." (3) To add emphasis to any of them, you can:

1. Use **their butts** or **their asses** as the object of the verb: "Wow, we really creamed their butts!"

2. Add **the heck/hell/crap/shit out of** between the verb and the object. Remember that **hell** and **crap** are sometimes offensive and that **shit** is usually offensive: "We slaughtered the heck out of 'em."

These verbs are often used in talk about sports, but they can be used in any situation where competition, winning, and losing are involved:

That guy makes a good speech, but he's gonna get clobbered in the election.

I test-drove a new Charger yesterday, and that baby stomps all the competition.

Clobber, **stomp**, **whomp**, and **whup** all have the basic meaning of "hit" or "strike." (*Stomp* means "strike downward with the foot.") Many other verbs with the same basic meaning are used informally to talk about winning and losing, and they can all be used in the same patterns as the verbs above: **bash, beat, hammer, maul, pound, slam, thrash, wallop, whip.**

"The Lobos got mauled Friday night 28–7 by the Utah Utes."
"Michigan walloped Indiana 38–0 to win a spot in the play-offs."
"The last time the two teams met, the Huskies pounded the Mavericks 47–19."
"Pakistan got thrashed in the match against Western Australia."

These verbs can also be used to talk about any situation in which one person, group, or party attacks another. For example:
"U.S. forces pounded the Iraqi city of Fallujah overnight."
"The powerful blizzard has pounded the Rocky Mountains with three feet of snow."
"He can't believe how badly he got pounded in the debate."

In the comic strip at the beginning of the unit, did you notice the two questions that didn't look like questions ("Cause he sees we're gonna get smeared no matter what?" and "Action like us getting whomped with a 30-point spread?")? That's because they're actually opinions rather than real questions—but they sound like questions because the speaker's voice goes up at the end. This way of talking is very common among American young people, often when they're saying something that they think is obvious.

Try It!

Write two sentences about each situation below, using verbs from this unit. One of the sentences should be active and the other passive (with *get*).

EXAMPLE: Final Score: San Francisco 38, Detroit 10

San Francisco really smeared Detroit.

Detroit got thrashed by San Francisco.

1. A hurricane hits southern Florida.

_____

_____

2. Republicans lose the election.

_____

_____

3. Senator Laforge severely criticizes the press in a speech.

_____

_____

4. Oil prices rise and the stock market falls.

_____

_____

5. The citrus-fruit crop is damaged by frost.

_____

_____

What Kinda Place Is This?

Many slang words are used to describe places.

boonies /'buːniz/ *noun* rural areas far away from cities

crib *noun* the place where you live

dive *noun* a restaurant, bar, or club that is dirty or unpleasant

hole *noun* an unpleasant and undesirable place

hood *noun* neighborhood

joint *noun* a business open to the public, especially a small place of entertainment

pad *noun* the place where you live

cruise /'kruːz/ *verb* go

Let's blow this popsicle stand Let's leave this undesirable place.

I'm/We're outta here I'm/We're about to leave.

But sometimes when people talk about places, they aren't places that you could find on a map!

happy place *noun* a state of mind in which you feel happy and secure and nothing bothers you

go there experience or talk about something. Always used in negative expressions: "My date with Alex? Please! Don't go there!"

Different Ways of Living

There isn't any common slang verb meaning "reside, live in a place"; people just say "Where do you live?" or "Where are you living?" However, if you're only living somewhere for a short time, or if you're living with your girlfriend or boyfriend, slang comes to the rescue!

OK if I crash with you guys when I'm in town next weekend?

Sure, you can have Gina's room. She's been shacking up with this new guy she met.

crash with sb *phrasal verb* stay in someone's house or apartment for a short time

shack up with sb *phrasal verb* live with someone whom you're having sex with

Try It!

I. Using the word or expression in parentheses, write a sentence that is a good response to the questions or sentences below.

EXAMPLE: Seems like Anna is always in a bad mood these days. (*happy place*)

Yeah, she needs to find her happy place

1. What took you so long to get here? (*boonies*)

2. We ate at that new Mexican place in Parkton. (*dive*)

3. I thought Whitney was crashing with you guys. (*shack up with sb*)

4. Got time for a quick cup of coffee? (*be outta here*)

5. Wanna talk about what happened last night? (*go there*)

II. Many cities and other places in the United States have informal names that are often used in conversation and writing. Match up the city names on the left with their nicknames on the right. (You'll have to guess at some of them.)

CITY	NICKNAME
1. Boston ____	A. **Motown**
2. Chicago ____	B. **"inside the Beltway"**
3. Detroit ____	C. **Tinseltown**
4. Hollywood ____	D. **Philly**
5. Las Vegas ____	E. **Beantown**
6. Los Angeles ____	F. **the Big Apple**
7. New Orleans ____	G. **the Big Easy**
8. New York City ____	H. **LA**
9. Philadelphia ____	I. **Vegas**
10. San Francisco ____	J. **the Windy City**
11. Washington, D.C. ____	K. **Frisco**

Gimme Some Skin

Gimme some skin is a slang way to ask someone to shake hands. You learned some slang for parts of the body in Unit 25. Many other slang terms come from parts of the body, or things that you do with your body—or with someone else's body! (Some of the slang in this unit is quite offensive.) First, things to do with your hands:

High fives is a gesture that two people make, slapping their palms together in the air. People give high fives when they're happy, and especially when they have had a success.

If you **cop a feel**, you manage to touch someone in a sexual way that is probably offensive: "Some jerk standing next to me on the bus tried to cop a feel and I slapped him."

Holding your middle finger straight up, with the back of your hand toward someone, means "Fuck you." This gesture is called **flipping sb ⇄ off**, **flipping sb the bird**, or **giving sb the finger**. It is very offensive.

If you give someone a **snuggy** (or a **wedgie**), you pull up on the back of his underwear. This is only done as a joke to someone you know very well— even then he probably won't like it!

Next, a few things that people do with their bodies:

A **beaver shot** is a view up a woman's skirt or dress, especially if she has nothing on underneath. Many women find this term offensive, and it is used mainly by men: "When she bent down, like ten of us got a full-on beaver shot. Dude! No panties!"

If you **body-slam** someone, you hit him with your whole body: "He body-slammed the referee and got thrown out of the game." **Body slam** is also a noun: "I just elbowed him accidentally and he gave me a body slam."

When you **fart**, gas escapes from between your buttocks. Most people find the word offensive. A slangier way to say **fart** is **cut one**: "Rudy cut one in Math class today and we nearly had to leave the room."

Fart is also a noun: "He let a fart as he walked by my cube." **Cut a fart** is a slangier way to say "let a fart."

fart around *phrasal verb* waste time doing something unimportant: "Quit farting around and do some work."

If you **flash** someone, you show them your genitals by quickly uncovering them and then covering them again: "The weirdest thing I ever saw was when a 90-year-old woman flashed me at a picnic."

Someone who runs naked through a public place is a **streaker**. This activity is called **streaking**.

If you **moon** someone, or **shoot sb the moon**, you expose your buttocks to them. This is usually done as a joke or an insult.

Finally, some other slang inspired by our bodies:

Arm candy is a man or woman who you enjoy being seen in public with because he or she is so good-looking: "She's kind of a ditz, but she'll make good arm candy for the office Christmas party."

Your *armpit* is where your arm joins your body. When you say a place is the **armpit of sth**, you mean that it's a very undesirable place to live: "She lives in Coolidge, the armpit of southern Colorado."

The informal word for *navel* is **belly button**. Belly buttons are of two types: An **innie** goes inward like a small bowl, and an **outie** sticks outward.

Try It!

I. Make up sentences below in response to those given, using the words in parentheses.

1. What were all those cops doing on the football field? (*streaker*)

   _____

2. What happened to your arm? (*body slam*)

   _____

3. Describe your navel. (*belly button, innie or outie*)

   _____

4. Who's the guy with Jessica? (*arm candy*)

   _____

II. Many different slang expressions are formed by adding -*head* to the end of a noun. The new word usually describes a kind of person. Match up the definitions on the left with the -*head* words on the right. (You may have to use a dictionary.)

1. an intellectual ____	A. **airhead**
2. a stupid person ____	B. **jarhead**
3. a person who wears a turban (offensive) ____	C. **egghead**
4. a person who uses LSD ____	D. **acidhead**
5. a person who likes heavy-metal music ____	E. **dickhead**
6. a person who knows a lot about cars ____	F. **metalhead**
7. a person who is both stupid and annoying ____	G. **raghead**
8. a Marine ____	H. **gearhead**

Once you figure out which of these terms means "a stupid person," you can add to your vocabulary all the following words, which mean about the same thing: **blockhead, bonehead, bubblehead, fathead, knucklehead, thickhead.** (And remember **pinhead** from Unit 38.)

46 High Life

Many young people experiment with drugs and alcohol. You learned vocabulary in Unit 29 that was related to the criminal side of drug use; here's some new vocabulary to add to it:

blotto /'blɑːtoʊ/ *adjective* drunk

shit-faced *adjective* very drunk (may be offensive)

tanked *adjective* drunk

wasted *adjective* very drunk or strongly affected by drugs

acid *noun* LSD

booze *noun* liquor or other alcoholic drink

downer *noun* a barbiturate (a drug that makes you sleepy)

hash *noun* hashish (a drug related to marijuana)

Jell-O shot *noun* a small glassful of Jell-O dessert with alcohol in it

reefer *noun* marijuana; a marijuana cigarette

knock sth ⇄ back *phrasal verb* drink or eat something

toke up *phrasal verb* smoke hashish or marijuana

trip *verb* use LSD or some other hallucinogenic drug

There are many other slang words and expressions about using drugs and alcohol and their effects. Here are the most common ones:

Bombed, **loaded**, **smashed**, **soused** /ˈsaʊst/, and **plastered** are other words meaning "drunk." **Fucked up** (offensive) and **faded** can mean either "drunk" or "affected by drugs."

Pot and **weed** are other words for "marijuana." People who use marijuana regularly may also refer to it as **shit**: "Did you try that Mexican weed? That was totally great shit!" A marijuana cigarette is called a **joint**, a **reefer**, or a **dubb** if it is small and rolled in paper, or a **blunt** if it is fat or made from a cigar.

Speed and **uppers** are words for amphetamines, drugs that keep you awake and make your heart beat faster.

Coke is short for *cocaine*. (Also for *Coca-Cola*.) **Crack** is a strong form of cocaine. **Crack** is usually smoked in a special pipe; **coke** is **snorted**—that is, sucked up through the nose.

Someone seriously addicted to a drug that he injects into his veins is a **junkie**. The drug is usually heroin, which is sometimes called **junk**. Injecting a drug with a needle is called **shooting up**: "She started shooting up in high school and soon had a $100-a-day habit."

A HEAD FOR DRUGS

In the last unit you learned **acidhead**, a name for a person who uses LSD. Many words describing drug users are made from adding *-head* to the name of a drug: **cokehead**, **crackhead**, **pothead**, and **hashhead** all describe users of particular drugs. **Dopehead** is sometimes used as a general term for any drug user.

Try It!

Here's an account of a wild party in standard English. Write a new version, substituting slang words for all the underlined words. You can use vocabulary from this or previous units, or other words you may know.

There was a party last night at Marc's <u>house</u>. There were <u>many</u> people there and I didn't know anybody. <u>A young man</u> offered me a <u>marijuana cigarette</u> but I said <u>no</u>. In one corner some <u>women</u> were <u>drinking</u> shots of tequila and laughing. I walked toward them and then <u>an annoying person</u> grabbed my <u>buttocks</u> and said "Hey! Don't I know you?" <u>I told him that he didn't</u> and that he should keep his <u>hands</u> to himself. I was not liking this party. The music was <u>extremely</u> loud and there was nowhere to <u>relax</u>. I decided to <u>leave</u> and just as I got to the door <u>a group of men</u> walked in with guns. I think they were <u>drug addicts</u>. They said "Don't nobody move." This <u>scared me very much</u>. It got <u>very</u> quiet and then we heard someone in the kitchen on their cell phone—to the <u>police</u>. Next thing, <u>a woman who was very drunk</u> started screaming and one of the <u>drug addicts</u> told her to <u>be quiet</u>. She <u>became quiet very fast</u>. Then we heard sirens and two <u>police</u> cars pulled up. The robbers ran through the house, looking for a way out. Then the <u>police</u> caught two of the <u>drug addicts</u> inside, but they also <u>arrested another man</u> who was just at the party: they recognized him <u>because</u> apparently he was a <u>drug dealer</u> who had been running <u>an illegal cocaine operation</u>. Next time Marc invites me to a party I'm <u>going to say no</u>!

_____

_____

_____

_____

_____

_____

_____

_____

_____

_____

_____

_____

_____

_____

_____

_____

_____

4 Like I Care

You can say **Who cares?** to show that you're annoyed with what someone has said or asked, or that you think something isn't important. Expressions like this are used in many different ways.

Who gives a darn/hoot? has the same meaning as **Who cares?** People also say this using offensive words. **Who gives a damn?** is offensive to some people. **Who gives a shit?** is often offensive. You may hear **Who gives a fuck?** and **Who gives a rat's ass?**, but they're offensive and you shouldn't use them.

In conversation, you can show that you don't think something is important by beginning your sentence with "I don't care if . . ."

"I don't care if . . ." has different slang forms with the same meaning. You can say **I don't give a darn if . . .**, but you'll also hear this expression with offensive words (**I don't give a shit if . . .**, **I don't give a fuck if . . .**).

Another way to say the same thing is with a phrase that has many other uses:

We're really sorry you got fired, but we'll be so disappointed if you don't come back for the Christmas party!

Right. Whatever. Like I care.

People say **Like I care**, or sometimes **It's not like I care**, to emphasize that they don't care about something or think that it's important. **Like I care** is a somewhat rude way of saying "You think that I care, but I don't!"

When **like** is used to introduce a sentence (as in **Like I care**), it's an informal way of reversing the sentence's meaning. That is, it's often used *ironically* to express the opposite of what you mean or what is true:

Guess what—Tony and Gina are coming for the weekend too!

Great. Like we need two more people sleeping in the living room.

I promise I'll pay you back the money after I sell my car.

Like that will ever happen!

When someone says **Whatever** all by itself, it means the same thing as **Who cares?**

Try It!

I. Complete the responses to the sentences below, using expressions that you learned in this unit.

EXAMPLE: If you're hungry, you can have that last piece of pizza.

Like _____*there was any other*_____ choice!

1. Don't you think the tickets are a little pricey?

Who _____? Matt said he'd pay.

2. But it's really cold outside.

I don't _____ if it's 50 below zero—get out there and shovel the sidewalk!

3. I can't believe it! That puppy peed in every room of the house!

What, _____ it's supposed to know better?

II. Read each response below, then write a sentence that it might be responding to:

1. _____

Like you didn't spend the whole weekend sleeping!

2. _____

So who cares if they don't talk to me.

3. _____

She doesn't give a damn about her job.

122

48 In Deep Doo-Doo

Got troubles? Slang can help you through them!

Uh-oh! Do you see what I see?

Holy shit! Look at that humongous mess!

Man, we are in mega deep doo-doo.

Totally up a creek. How we gonna get outta here?

GARAGE

Dennis'll flip when he sees this. Who wants to fess up and take the heat?

Uh, hello! Why should we take the rap for it?

Can we pitch in on the towing bill?

Yeah, if it's not too ginormous.

humongous /hjuˈmʌŋgəs/ *adjective*
huge

mega /ˈmɛgə/ *adverb or adjective*
extremely, very; huge

Uh-oh /ˈʌˌoʊ/ *exclamation* used when something bad has happened or is about to happen.

in deep doo-doo in serious trouble. A stronger way of saying this is **in deep shit**, which may be offensive.

up a creek in serious trouble. A stronger way of saying this is **up shit creek**, which may be offensive.

ginormous /dʒaɪˈnoɚˈməs/ *adjective*
huge

fess up *phrasal verb* confess; admit to doing something

pitch in on sth *phrasal verb* participate equally, share the cost of something

take the heat accept blame

Hello! *exclamation* A sarcastic response to indicate that someone has just said something stupid.

Humongous probably comes from *huge* and *monstrous*. **Ginormous** is made up from parts of two words. What do you think they are?

pricey /ˈpraɪsi/ *adjective* expensive

big-time *adverb and adjective* to a high degree; a lot

a quick buck *noun* money that can be made quickly and easily

vibe, vibes *noun* a feeling you get from your surroundings or from another person

cough up *phrasal verb* pay

patch sth ⇄ up *phrasal verb* repair something quickly and often carelessly

pop for sth *phrasal verb* pay for something; buy something

spring for sth *phrasal verb* pay for something

stick sb with sth *phrasal verb* make someone pay or be responsible for something unfairly

totaled *adjective* completely wrecked so that it isn't worth repairing

be out to do sth intend to do something

in spades a lot; to a high degree

no biggie it isn't a big deal; it isn't important

Try It!

The story below is missing some important adverbs and prepositions. Fill in the blanks with words from the list below. You may use some words more than once, and other words not at all.

back   down   for   in   off   on   out   up

Here's what's really got me _____. Last week when I was cruisin' in the burbs, some lowlife dirtball plowed into me at a red light. The sucker didn't have any insurance! Boy, was I ticked _____! Now somehow I've gotta pop _____ the repairs myself. I'm totally broke. I tried to hit _____ my girlfriend but she's all tapped _____. Everybody else just bags _____ me. This will set me _____ 500 bucks! How am I gonna cough _____ that amount?

49 Tough Nuts to Crack

A **tough nut to crack** is a person or thing that's difficult to understand or deal with, or a problem that's hard to solve. Some slang is like this! Sometimes the words are easy to understand but the meaning is difficult. And sometimes you know what the words mean but you don't quite understand how they're being used.

I'm not goin' anywhere with you in that funky ride.

Let's go to that funky new jazz café. The food's really good.

I love the way Ashley always wears those funky clothes.

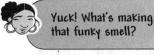

Yuck! What's making that funky smell?

Funky is a good example of a slang word that has different meanings.

When people describe certain things as **funky**, the meaning is negative: **funky** smells and moods are unpleasant, and a **funky** car or appliance is usually an old one with many problems. But when clothing, hairstyles, or music is described as **funky**, it means original, creative, and unusual.

Bad sometimes means "bad" and sometimes means "good." How can you tell the difference? There are two things to watch for. When **bad** means "good," people usually pronounce it with strong emphasis and there's no adverb (like *really, pretty, very,* or *totally*) in front of it:

"Check out this new single from Ja Rule—it is *bad!*" (= good)
"Didja hear Ja Rule's new single? It's pretty bad." (= bad)

phat /ˈfæt/ *adjective* attractive and pleasing

Fat and **phat** have the same pronunciation but different meanings. When they're spoken, you have to decide what the speaker means!

ONE BADASS MOFO

Another word that sounds as if it might be negative but usually is positive is **badass** /ˈbædˌæs/. **Badass** can be a noun or an adjective. It means someone or something that is powerful and impressive, perhaps someone you would respect and fear more than you would like: "Clint Eastwood plays this badass cowboy." Some people find it offensive.

Mofo /ˈmoʊˌfoʊ/ is a short form of another slang word, **motherfucker**. **Motherfucker** is a very strong and offensive insult. However, **mofo** is sometimes used in a friendly way among young black men. And calling someone a **badass mofo** is usually a compliment: it suggests that he's mean but powerful.

Short and Sweet

Slang often uses short and very common words together.

Come look at and **go get** are informal ways of saying "come and look at" and "go and get." When another common verb follows *come* or *go*, you don't need *and* between them: "Come listen to this new song," "Go see who's at the door."

How come is an informal way of asking "why."

Get it is an informal way of saying "understand."

Try It!

You decide: Is the underlined word in these sentences saying something good or something bad? Write another word—either slang or standard English—that could take the place of the underlined word.

EXAMPLE: Phew! Who left these <u>funky</u> socks on the coffee table? *smelly*

1. That's a <u>bad</u> suit, bro! How much you pay for it? _____

2. I bought these <u>funky</u> '70s disco records last week. _____

3. Oh, I get it. You're in such a <u>funky</u> mood today. _____

4. Who knew her singing would be so incredibly <u>bad</u>? _____

5. How come you got the new toaster and I got this <u>funky</u> one? _____

6. Come check out this CD—it's got some <u>bad</u> tracks on it. _____

See Ya

Catch ya later!

See ya!

Hasta la vista!

Ciao!

There are many informal ways to say good-bye; the four in the illustration are some of the most common ones.

Hasta la vista /ˌɑːstɑlɑˈviːstɑ/ is Spanish for *good-bye*.

When people are parting from each other for a long or indefinite time, they sometimes say

So long /soʊˈlɑːŋ/

Five-Minute Warning

Before you say good-bye, you often want to say something to indicate that you're going, or that you're ready to leave. Slang provides many different ways of doing this. **I'm outta here** means that you're leaving—or ready to leave—immediately. Other slang verbs can be used to suggest to the person with you that it's time to leave:

Let's blow/book/bounce/get/jam/roll/went Let's go: "Hey, let's went already—we're late!"

bone out *phrasal verb* leave: "I'm fixin' to bone out."

buzz off *phrasal verb* leave: "She just buzzed off without saying anything."

take off *phrasal verb* leave: "Come say good-bye before you take off."

mosey /ˈmoʊzi/ leave (**mosey** also means "go slowly")

scram *verb* leave quickly: "You better scram before I clobber you."

skedaddle /skɪˈdædl̩/ *verb* leave quickly: "We saw who was there and skedaddled."

split *verb* leave: "They split about an hour ago."

vamoose /vəˈmuːs/ *verb* leave quickly: "Better vamoose before they get here."

A *transcript* is the written record of exactly what someone has said. When a transcript is accurate, it almost always includes slang, errors, and expressions that don't add any meaning. Read this transcript of a man talking about the end of his friend's marriage:

Um, obviously it was going through some heavy weather. Whether it was going to end or not we don't know. I mean all marriages go through their ups and downs. Divorce? I mean, he never flat out said anything like that or any suggestion of it to me, you know. I mean, it's like, you know, when you are friends with someone there are like way subtler forms of information transfer than just flat out talking, right? I mean, it's like, I'm just saying it's like, why did he need to tell me? I mean, the thing is it's like, the time he would have been communicating any sorta, you know, sense that he wanted to leave her was when they came back from Hawaii, when I kinda didn't see him, you know. I don't think he was like planning to leave her at that point necessarily, I mean, I don't know though. You know, well 'cos there was super pressure on him to go through counseling. His wife is telling him he totally needs to go through treatment, his boss, his family, you know. So he goes and he tries to get off drugs and he can't or he doesn't want to. I mean it's like basically he doesn't want to 'cos it's like, you know, there is no reason for him to get off drugs. I mean, it's not like he's poverty-stricken and robbing grocery stores to supply his habit. She was the one who was all gung-ho for him to quit but she couldn't quit herself. I mean, the most ridiculous example was one time he called me up to get some speed and then the other line rang and I answered it and it was her asking me to get her some dope, and I was like, hello?

Now look at the same speech with the extra words removed:

Obviously it was going through some heavy weather. Whether it was going to end or not we don't know. All marriages go through their ups and downs. Divorce? He never said anything like that or any suggestion of it to me. When you are friends with someone there are subtler forms of information transfer than just talking. Why did he need to tell me? The time he would have been communicating any sense that he wanted to leave her was when they came back from Hawaii, when I didn't see him. I don't think he was planning to leave her at that point. There was pressure on him to go through counseling. His wife is telling him he needs to go through treatment, his boss, his family. So he goes and he tries to get off drugs and he can't or he doesn't want to. He doesn't want to 'cos there is no reason for him to get off drugs. It's not like he's poverty-stricken and robbing grocery stores to supply his habit. She was the one who was all gung-ho for him to quit but she couldn't quit herself. The most ridiculous example was one time he called me up to get some speed and then the other line rang and it was her asking me to get her some dope.

In conversation, people use many short words and phrases that don't add any meaning to a sentence. (You learned a few of these in Unit 7.) These often aren't truly slang, but they're only used in informal speech. Here are the words and phrases from the transcript above that add no meaning:

ah

uh

um

kinda

sorta

you know

I don't know

I mean

the thing is

I'm just saying

it's like

When the speaker says **right?** at the end of a sentence, it means that he wants to know if you agree with him (though he doesn't actually wait for an answer). He twice uses another term, **flat out**, which means "actually" or "absolutely."

Like, What Else?

The speaker uses **like** in two different ways. Both are extremely common in informal speech, but not in writing.

1. *as an adverb:* **Like** is often used before adverbs: "I know it's like way late, but can I come over to your place?" It's also often used before verbs: "We walked in the door and the kids were like jumping all over the furniture." And also before adjectives: "There were only like twenty kids there." "The whole show was just, like, incredible!" In all these uses, **like** may have no meaning at all! If it means anything, it usually suggests that there's something approximate or uncertain about what the speaker is saying.

2. *with am/are/is to mean "say" or "said":* "So she's like, 'How do you do that?' and I'm like, 'I dunno, it just happens.'" Here, "I'm like" and "she's like" mean "I said" and "she said." These expressions are extremely common among young people, who often use them to show that they're telling you in their own words rather than in the exact words that were used.

You will hear these uses of **like** a great deal, but you probably shouldn't use them. If you do, people may think you haven't learned English properly!

How Some Folks Talk

Slang is very popular in movies. In fact, *every* movie about modern life uses slang. Movies are a good place to learn how slang sounds. Watching English-language movies on DVD, with the English subtitles visible, is an excellent way to learn how slang is pronounced.

The dialogue in the box below, between a man (Ordell) and a woman (Jackie), is from a movie by Quentin Tarantino called *Jackie Brown*. This conversation takes place in a bar, when the two characters are discussing a plan they have to catch some criminals. See how much you can understand:

ORDELL: I gotta remember this place. This is all right. Two minutes from your crib, ten minutes from your work. I bet you come here on a Saturday night, you need nigga repellent keep 'em off your ass.

JACKIE: I do okay.

ORDELL: You a fine lookin' woman, Jackie. I bet you do a damn sight better than okay. You think anybody followed you?

JACKIE: I don't think so, but it don't really matter. They know I'm meeting you.

ORDELL: How the fuck they know that?

JACKIE: I told them.

ORDELL: You told em? You told em it's me?

JACKIE: They already know it's you.

ORDELL: Well, shit. That don't mean you gotta confirm it!

JACKIE: Look, the only way I can get permission to fly is if I agree to help them. Which is what I have to appear to be doing. So I give them something they already know. You.

ORDELL: Didja tell 'em anything else?

JACKIE: I told them you got a half a million dollars in Mexico, and you want me to bring it here.

ORDELL: You told 'em that?

JACKIE: It's true, isn't it?

ORDELL: What the fuck's that got to do with it?

JACKIE: They know I'm delivering for you. I mention the half-million 'n' they don't give a fuck about that— they want you with guns. So I say, well, if you want proof he's getting paid for selling them, let me bring the money in.

As you see, Ordell starts by telling Jackie that she must attract a lot of men when she comes to this bar. Jackie says that, in order to win the trust of the federal agents, she told them that she is meeting Ordell, and that Ordell wants her to smuggle $500,000 from Mexico. If you were Ordell, would you trust Jackie?

THE N-WORD

Another highly offensive word is **nigger**, an insulting form of *negro*, which is an old-fashioned word for a dark-skinned person whose ancestors were African. Some African-Americans use **nigger** (or **nigga**) in rap songs or when they are speaking among themselves, but no one else should ever use it.

Hundreds of complete movie screenplays can be found on the Web. If you have a favorite English-language movie and you want to study its language, just type "screenplays" into a search engine.

Try It!

You probably noticed that Ordell leaves out many auxiliary verbs and some other small words. In each of the following sentences, write the word or words that are required in order to make the sentence standard English.

1. I gotta remember this place.

   I _____ got to remember this place.

2. You need nigga repellent keep 'em off your ass.

   You need nigga repellent _____ keep them off your ass.

3. You a fine lookin' woman, Jackie.

   You _____ a fine-looking woman, Jackie.

4. How the fuck they know that?

   How the fuck _____ they know that?

5. That don't mean you gotta confirm it.

   That doesn't mean you _____ to confirm it.

They're Playin' Yer Song!

The words of songs are called *lyrics*. You will usually hear lyrics rather than read them, but they always exist in written form as well.

As long as people have been singing in English, slang has been a part of it. At right are some words from an old folk song.

> Well I married me a wife, she give me trouble all my life,
> Run me out in the cold rain and snow.
> . . .
> Well I ain't got no use for your red apple juice,
> And I ain't gonna be treated this a-way.

You can see slang and nonstandard English in these two verses, such as **ain't**, **gonna**, and incorrect verb tenses. "This a-way" means simply "in this way." "Run me out in" means "She drove me out of the house into." The meaning of "I ain't got no use for your red apple juice" isn't completely clear.

Popular songs today also use a lot of slang, and different kinds of songs use different kinds of slang. Two kinds of music popular today—country music and hip-hop (rap)—use a lot of slang that may not be easy to understand at first.

> Now I got a gal that's sweet to me,
> She just ain't what she used to be.
> Just a little high headed,
> That's plain to see.
> Don't get above your raisin',
> Stay down on earth with me.
>
> Now lookee here, gal, don't you high-hat me.
> I ain't forgot what you used to be
> When you didn't have nothing,
> That was plain to see.
> Don't get above your raisin',
> Stay down on earth with me.

Lookin' at Country

Country music (or *country and Western music*) is popular music traditionally performed by white musicians from the American South and West. Country-music lyrics use many words and expressions that are mainly used by people who live in those regions and outside of cities. At left are some of the lyrics to "Don't Get Above Your Raising" by Lester Flatt. Here, **your raisin'** means "the way you were raised"—that is, the social or financial situation of your family.

gal *noun* girl, woman

high-hat *verb* act as if you are better than someone else

lookee here look here; pay attention to what I'm saying

133

I Dig Your Rap

Hip-hop and rap lyrics, on the other hand, use a lot of newer slang that comes from black American culture. Here's part of "Into You" by the singer Fabolous:

> But girl, I'ma do whatever just to keep a grin on you now.
>
> Where I roll, they wear bikinis in the winter too now.
>
> What you think about tan lines on the skin of you now?
>
> Why wouldn't I wanna spend a few thou
>
> On Fifth Ave, shopping sprees and them dinners to chow?
>
> I ain't concerned with other men would do now,
>
> As long as when I slide up in you, you growl.
>
> And any dude with you, he better be a kin of you now.
>
> And I ain't jealous, it's the principle now.
>
> I'm so into you

I'ma, **imma** / aɪmə, ɑːmə/ a contraction of *I'm* and *gonna* (which are already contractions!). So **I'ma** means "I am going to." This word is very common in rap lyrics.

Ave /æv/ the written abbreviation of *Avenue*, which is sometimes also pronounced in this short-ened form. (Fifth Avenue is a large avenue in New York City with expensive shops.)

This song has a few other lines that might be confusing. "Whatever just to keep a grin on you now" means "whatever is necessary to keep you smiling." "Where I roll" means "where I spend time." "Tan lines" are marks on the skin where the sun has tanned it. "I ain't concerned with other men would do" means "I'm not concerned with *what* other men would do." The seventh line is about sex. "Better" is short for "had better," which means "would be wise to," and "kin" means "relative," so "any dude with you, he better be a kin of you now" is a threat against any man who is seen talking to her but isn't related to her. When he says "it's the principle now," he means that talking to someone else's girlfriend violates a principle, or rule of conduct, in his society.

Studying lyrics can be one of the most enjoyable ways to learn new slang! Is there a song in English that you hear all the time but whose words you still can't understand? Learning a song's lyrics is easier than you think—sometimes you just need to see them written down. The lyrics of nearly all popular songs are on the Web.

Try It!

Think of a song you like, then go to any search engine and type in "lyrics" and the title of your song (with quotation marks around the title). Identify all the slang words and expressions in your song.

Let Your Fingers Do the Talkin'

The Internet and handy electronic devices allow you to communicate with your friends—and with people that you may never meet! It used to be unusual to use slang with people who you didn't know very well, but the Internet has changed this. People who have conversations online usually use slang. Here are some places where people communicate and "talk" online:

BLOGS: Today one of the best places to find written slang is in blogs—diaries and journals that people keep on the Internet. Blogs are mostly written by young people, and they are often written in slang. Blogs can be found at many different sites, and many sites also give you the opportunity to write a blog of your own. Some of the most popular blogging sites are:

www.blogger.com	*www.movabletype.org*	*www.livejournal.com*
www.joeuser.com	*www.typepad.com*	*www.myspace.com*
www.flickr.com	*www.facebook.com*	*www.xanga.com*

GROUPS: An Internet group (or *newsgroup*) is a site devoted to a particular subject, where you can ask a question, answer a question, or express an opinion. Some groups, especially groups that deal with popular culture and personal matters, provide a good opportunity to read and write slang. Here are some sites where you can find a huge number of groups:

www.groups.yahoo.com	*www.groups.google.com*
www.groups.msn.com	*www.lsoft.com/catalist.html*

CHAT ROOMS: A chat room is a Web site where you can join an online conversation. Chat-room conversations happen in *real time;* as soon as you send your message, it appears on other people's screens, and anyone can type a response immediately. Conversations sometimes go extremely fast. Many people visit chat rooms in order to find someone to have sex with, but it's also possible to have friendly and interesting conversations in a chat room. You can find chat rooms at many different sites, including www.chat.yahoo.com and www.icq.com/icqchat.

TEXTING: If you have a cell phone (mobile phone), you probably know about texting already. It's a way to send a message to a friend's phone, using as few words and letters as possible. Texting uses some special language, which is easy to understand when you study it a little bit.

INSTANT MESSAGING: When you and your friends are online, you can type a message that they will see right away. These messages sometimes look like texting—but only if you're being a little bit lazy, because when you send instant messages, you usually have a full keyboard to work with!

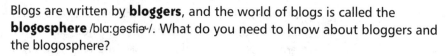

Blog Style

Blogs are written by **bloggers**, and the world of blogs is called the **blogosphere** /blɑ:ɡəsfiə/. What do you need to know about bloggers and the blogosphere?

There is no censorship. When you read blogs, you should be prepared to find a lot of offensive language—language that you should never use in polite conversation or formal writing. People also express their opinions freely in blogs, so don't be surprised to find very strong feelings.

There is often no editing. Some people write very carefully in their blogs and perhaps even use a spell-checker, but many others do not. You'll find misspelled words, grammatical errors, and sentences that don't always seem to make sense.

Bloggers love to shorten things. You have already learned many words that are shortened from longer words. Because many bloggers don't type very fast, their blogs often contain even shorter versions of some words. You'll learn about these in the next few units.

Bloggers often write the way they talk. Written language doesn't always let you express yourself as fully as speech, so blog writers sometimes add features to their writing to show how they would say something. We will look at the ways they do this in the coming units.

Many bloggers write about their everyday lives. Here's a blog from a young woman who has been looking for a job. Read all of it first and see how much you can understand.

---

got a 2nd interview w/ the guy i interviewed with on friday. check this job out-

#1 - it's a real estate development firm. been doin business for 20+ yrs & is obviously doing well b/c the office is GORGEOUS. oh my gosh. ive never seen a classier place. i mean yall—they had actual elevator music playing in the elevator. no joke. i stepped on that bitch & felt waaaay underdressed. so this gig wld require way formal business drag evryday which wld require a complete new wardrobe for me.

#2 - it's a receptionist job that sounds incredibly easy. answer phones. smile @ ppl. occasional administrative support, taking dictation, filing stuff, yada yada yada. directing clients to the conference room which is right next to my office. makin sure they have hot coffee & donuts.... sumthin is tellin me that i'd really REALLY hate that part of the job.
so.
w/ alla this in mind, i cld be faced w/ choosing b/t this gig and the Atlanta gig. maybe. i still havent been offered anything yet. but if i had to choose, i think ive come to the difficult conclusion that i'd go w/ the Atlanta gig. i'd be workin closer to my field of study, way more laid-back atmosphere (the corporate world is so not for me). and even tho the pay is 50 cent less, there's still opp'ty for cash bonuses. wish the benefits were better tho. and no servin any flamin coffee & damn donuts to nobody.

Let's look at some sentences in this blog, along with their "translation" into standard English.

got a 2nd interview = I got a second interview

Notice that the writer leaves out the subject of the sentence, which is "I," and writes "2nd" rather than "second" (because it's faster to type!). Many other writing shortcuts are used here, such as "@" for "at," "&" for "and," and "+" for "plus."

w/ the guy i interviewed with on friday = with the man who interviewed me on Friday

The abbreviation **w/** stands for *with*. This blogger doesn't capitalize words that are always capitalized in standard English (like *I* and *Friday*); this is common in blogs.

How about this sentence?

been in the republic building for 20+ yrs & is obviously doing well b/c the office is GORGEOUS.

Here the blogger types "gorgeous" in capital letters for emphasis; if she were speaking, she would be saying "gorgeous" loud and slowly. She again omits the subject of the sentence, and also part of the verb. What two words belong at the beginning of the sentence? And what word does **b/c** stands for?

Are you ready? Here's the standard English version:

It has been in the Republic Building for more than 20 years and is obviously doing well because the office is beautiful.

Here's another difficult section:

i stepped on that bitch & felt waaaay underdressed. so this gig wld require way formal business drag evryday which wld require a complete new wardrobe for me.

A **gig** is usually a job for a musician or entertainer, but here it just means "job." **Drag** usually means women's clothing when it is worn by a man, but here it just means clothing for a particular purpose. What is she referring to when she says "that bitch"?

People sometimes emphasize words by lengthening them when they speak. So when the blogger writes "way" as **waaaay**, she is emphasizing it.

The second sentence uses the abbreviation **wld**. What word does this stand for?

Are you ready for the standard English version?

I stepped onto the elevator and felt very underdressed. So this job would require very formal business dress every day, which would require a complete new wardrobe for me.

Look at the last paragraph of the blog entry above. Remember: The writer has had two interviews, one with a real-estate firm and one with a company in Atlanta. Write a standard English version of the last paragraph. Then answer the questions below.

_____

_____

_____

_____

_____

_____

_____

_____

_____

_____

_____

_____

_____

_____

1. Which job is more attractive: the one in Atlanta, or the one with the real estate firm?

   _____

2. Which job pays better? _____

3. Which job offers a more relaxed working environment? _____

Trippin'

You learned one meaning of the verb **trip** in Unit 46: that is, to take the drug LSD or some other strong drug. This meaning is related to several other slang meanings of **trip** and **tripping**. Here are some pieces from blogs that will help you understand the different ways that people **trip**.

A

I called my girlfriend one afternoon. Her roommate answers. I asked to speak to my girl ... her roommate tells me to hold on ... I hear some whisperin' and shit ... and then her roommate says "She ain't here. Bye." And hangs up on a playa!! WTF???? So while I'm sitting there wondering what's happenin, the phone rings. It's her, my girl. She launches into this bullshit about how things ain't workin out and how she's too young for me. This blows me away!! Then I start goin all soft inside, sayin "Buh-buh-but I love you! Whatcha mean it's over???"

And just as I'm reaching my peak of bein' a crybaby, guess who comes to my crib... my homies!! My mom let them in.

My girl finally hangs up on me, and I turn around and WHAM!!! My two best friends are standing RIGHT THERE!!! And then one of says, "What's wrong with you??? And I said, "Man, my girl broke up with me."

So then my boys say "why you trippin over some girl that we knew all along wasn't gonna work out... Man, you gotta stop all that cryin' an' shit."

When you're **tripping**, you're so emotional about something that you can't see it clearly. Here are some other words he uses:

homey /hoʊmi/ (plural: **homies**) *noun* a friend; a person you spend a lot of time with

playa /plejə/, **player** a man who is popular with women and dates a lot of them

WTF *abbreviation* for **What the fuck?** (see Unit 27). The abbreviation isn't offensive to most people, but the full form can be!

work out *phrasal verb* be successful. If you **work sth ⇄ out**, you find a way to make it successful or to finish it.

blow sb away *phrasal verb* amaze

And "Buh-buh-but" just means that he's stuttering with emotion when he tries to say "but."

Here's another example from a blogger writing about a different experience with a woman:

B

> alright...i'm at work (Subway) and i see this really cute chick by herself. She gets her food and sits down. i go out to the front to wipe tables — hey, it's my job, right? i smile at her and she smiles back. then, i go to the back. so, i start making some good eye contact w/ her, and i succeed. and all of a sudden she grabs her cell and makes a phone call, she freakin talked the rest of the time she was there, geez! So, what's the dilly? was it a pity smile, cuz i work at a food place? or was she just being nice (i doubt it)? is it that bad dating a guy that works for minimum wage? So i'm trippin out on all this and then don't even notice there's a customer trying to make an order.

As you see, this guy isn't very proud of working in a fast-food restaurant like Subway. When he says "hey, it's my job, right?" it means that he knows how little respect his readers have for this kind of job. Then he wonders if she smiled only because she pitied him. "Minimum wage" is the lowest wage that the state permits an employer to pay. "Eye contact" is when two people are looking at each other at the same time.

cell *noun* a cell phone

cuz *abbreviation* because

What's the dilly? = What's the deal? What's the situation?

Sometimes people use **tripping** to mean **ego-tripping**. People **on an ego-trip** think that they're greater, more important, or more intelligent than they really are:

> i'd just like to announce that i am a master of showin people how predictable they are. i swear to god sometimes my word is just law, and sooner or later they come back and i get to say i told you so. i'm not tripping, just tellin you how it is.

"**I swear to god**" means "I truly believe." "My word" here means "what I say." If you say "**I told you so**" to someone else, it means that something you said in the past has been shown to be correct. Do you believe him when he says he's not tripping?

> My hip-hop knowledge, however extensive (I'm trippin'), is still incomplete.

This blogger is saying that his knowledge of hip-hop music is large but not absolutely complete. "I'm trippin'" here means that "I'm boasting."

A **power trip** is similar to an **ego trip**. Someone who is **power-tripping** or **on a power trip** likes to control other people, as you can see from these bloggers:

> this power-tripping cop pulled us over and stuck the mother of all flashlights right in my eyes.

> the student senate is a buncha power-tripping little kids enjoying (probably) the last elected office they will ever hold.

> We have a new boss at work. She's a bitch and is on a power trip.

You already know **pull over**. When someone says "**the mother of all _____**," it means "the biggest of all _____."

Guilt-tripping is a special kind of tripping. When you **guilt-trip some-body** or **lay a guilt trip on somebody**, you try to make the person feel guilty, so that he or she will do something you want:

> Nearly 200 e-mail messages stacked up while I was gone, and folks are guilt-tripping me for not getting back to them.

> Anyway, he's guilt-tripping me into putting him into the "Sites I Like" section of my blog, which I'm not going to do.

> First she blew me off on Thursday, then she tried to lay a guilt trip on me for not sticking around for her on Friday.

blow sb/sth ⇄ off *phrasal verb* ignore or abandon someone; fail to appear somewhere after telling someone that you would

stick around *phrasal verb* stay in one place, wait

So do you get it? The main idea of **tripping** is having something in your mind that prevents you from behaving normally.

Some people now use **tripped** as an adjective:

> i have one day to pack . . . and im leaving saturday night. im kinda tripped about this . . . and im scared about the plane ride...

When **tripping** is used about things instead of people, it means "out of order" or "not behaving properly":

> I had to have the tech guy check out my monitor, it was tripping and wldnt display the menus right.

> At the moment, this website is trippin' and I can't get my photos to upload.

Try It!

1. **Read passage A again. Then write one or two paragraphs, using informal English and slang, about a time when you were tripping about something and your friends pointed it out to you.**

   _____

   _____

   _____

   _____

   _____

2. **Read passage B again, then write a short paragraph, using informal English and slang, to explain why you think the woman didn't show more interest in this man. If you like, you can comment on his ideas about why she wasn't interested.**

   _____

   _____

   _____

   _____

   _____

3. **Write answers to these questions, based on your own experiences:**

   When was the last time someone blew you off?

   _____

   _____

   When was the last time you blew something off? Why?

   _____

   _____

   Have you ever tried to guilt-trip someone? What was it about?

   _____

   _____

   Give an example of someone who you think is on a power trip. What did the person do to make you think this?

   _____

   _____

56 Vibin'

Some common words have special slang meanings that describe ways that people feel or behave. Read these entries from blogs and see if you can understand the underlined words.

Erica called and asked me to come over for a band practice but i couldn't get a ride. i really wanted to go hang out with them, but i'm not feeling TOTALLY <u>together</u> so it's probably better i get to sit here in my pajamas.

Jermaine has got to <u>get his shit together</u> before he loses this job. He was totally wasted and <u>out of it</u> yesterday, and he wasn't really <u>with it</u> this morning either.

There was all sorts of insane explosions going on all around us. I've never felt fear like this. I was like, this is it, I'm gonna die. I cannot put into words how scared I was. The vehicle in front of us got hit 3 times. I kind of <u>lost it</u> and I was yelling and screaming all sorts of things.

Today i had my 2nd crazy menstrual woman mood swing in my history of egg makin. and yall i didnt even realize it till it was over. I'm at work, talkin to my favorite person on IM and we're talkin about the silliest kinda shit, right, i mean we may as wella been discussin which breakfast cereal is worthy of bein eaten for lunch and i got so <u>worked up</u>. over nothing! n o t h i n g ! and yall i just wld not let the shit die and i swear to god i was rational and logical and right in my mind at the time.

I decided to go ahead and get a viola to bring the notes down a bit lower. I keep looking over at it, knowing that I am about to start <u>vibin'</u> with it and making music. I will really be <u>in the zone</u> when I have the house to myself for a minute and no one is listening.

Went to a party at Willa's house and danced with her a bit, but she is <u>hard to read</u> and I don't quite know if she is <u>vibing</u> me back or maybe I am just <u>off my game</u> and she doesn't even like me at all.

All of the underlined words and expressions are ways to talk about people's internal feelings or ideas.

together *adjective* mentally and emotionally balanced; sensible and capable

143

worked up *predicate adjective* upset and angry

get your shit together organize yourself so that you're able to meet your responsibilities. It may be offensive; a more polite way to say it is **get your act together**.

in the zone feeling very good and able to achieve something very well

lose it lose control of your behavior or emotions. It often means "become uncontrollably angry," but not here.

off your game not able to work, perform, or communicate as well as usual. Less strong than **out of it**.

out of it not able to work or communicate well; not "together"

with-it able to work or communicate effectively; the opposite of **out of it**

hard to read difficult to understand

"Band practice" means practice for a marching band in high school or college, and a "mood swing" is a quick change in a person's mood.

In Unit 48 you learned the noun **vibe** (or **vibes**), meaning a feeling that you get from your surroundings. **Vibe** is also used as a verb. Look at the last two examples of it above, and at these next two:

> We just lounge around each other's rooms in our birthday suits, just <u>vibin' off</u> of each other's male forms and hairy chests writing and posting what we think is hilarious that day.

> This guy is too cool for me but when i went with my sister and he was my cashier my sister was like "dude, that guy was <u>vibing</u> you in a big way!". of course when i asked if i should go out with him, she said "fuck no! you need a guy who is a professional, someone who is educated, not some record store guy!"

If you **vibe with** or **vibe off** someone or something, you are completely in harmony with them and enjoying what you are doing with them. If you **vibe** someone, you communicate something to them with your behavior, rather than telling them in words what you mean.

"In our birthday suits" means "with no clothes on" (that is, just the way you were born). "Posting" means writing things for an Internet group site (see Unit 58). In the last example, a girl calls her own sister "**Dude**," even though **Dude** is normally used for guys.

Try It!

Read all the blog passages above again, making sure that you understand the new words. Then write a paragraph on each of the topics below, using as many words and expressions from this unit as you can.

1. Describe your experience of trying to decide whether someone you met is romantically interested in you.

   _____

   _____

   _____

   _____

   _____

   _____

   _____

2. Describe a time when you didn't understand what was happening in a social situation, and how you tried to find out.

   _____

   _____

   _____

   _____

   _____

   _____

3. List several activities that make you feel really good—things you like to do because you do them well and find them rewarding.

   _____

   _____

   _____

   _____

   _____

   _____

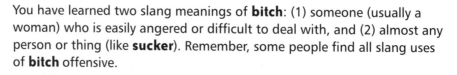

Bitchin'

You have learned two slang meanings of **bitch**: (1) someone (usually a woman) who is easily angered or difficult to deal with, and (2) almost any person or thing (like **sucker**). Remember, some people find all slang uses of **bitch** offensive.

Bitch can also be a verb, meaning "complain." Complaining is something that people do best in their blogs! But bloggers usually try to make their complaints funny so that other people will enjoy reading them.

This blogger sees an advertisement on a train that really annoys her:

> I'm on the blue line headed downtown (standing again because I NEVER get a friggin seat) and I look up to see this ad on my train. The ad has a black dude on it somewhere on the 'streets of Chicago' talking on his cell phone, and there's a black lady in the background. I guess this was supposed to be his 'love interest' once he got off the phone.
>
> You would think this would be an ad about a cell phone or something. He could have said to his boy "Man, I'm glad I have my Sprint wireless cell phone here. It gives me great reception so I can ask you how to lay the mack down on this honey over there." Or maybe cologne. He could have said, "Man, I'm so glad I bought this Axe body spray for men." You know - so he'll smell good when he puts the mack down. But nooooo. What did he say? This man says to his boy.....on his cell phone......with the honey in view........"Man, I'm so glad I got that syphilis test."
>
> W......T.......F??????? Are you serious? Syphilis? First of all, who does that? What playa would leave the clinic, call his boy immediately, and declare victory over syphilis as a reason for being able to lay the mack down to the black lady in the background? I see. I see what yall were trying to do, but come on! Whoever came up with that hot mess needed to take it back to the drawing board.

This blogger claims to be amazed and outraged that an attractive advertisement is actually telling people to get tested for a sexual disease. You already know most of the slang here, including **friggin'**, **WTF**, **playa**, and **y'all**. "The blue line" is a subway route that is colored blue on the city's subway map, and "body spray" is a good-smelling deodorant. You can guess that "nooooo" is just an emphatic way of saying "no," and "his boy" here just means "his friend." Taking something "back to the drawing board" means redesigning it. Here are two new slang terms:

honey *noun* an attractive woman or man

put the mack down = lay the mack down (see Unit 37)

The next blogger had experiences in some bars that he didn't enjoy:

After we got boozed up, the next stop was the Canteen. This place is always filled with your typical dirty hippies. They even have dirty hippy bands playing so that all the dirty hippies can dance and swing their shitlocks around. I was kinda tired of the hippies on this particular night, so we went across the street to a disgusting shithole of a place called Tony's. If you've ever been to the other local shitholes around here, you'll know what I'm talking about. While these places certainly suck, Tony's takes the cake in that department. Some drunk redneck wouldn't let us take even ONE of the chairs at his EMPTY six person table because "someone was sitting there." So we shot him the hairy eyeball until his other five redneck friends came back from macking on mullet-headed whores. I imagined them running to their pickups to grab their 30.6s off the rack and returning to give us a typical redneck-style beatdown. We took the secret entrance out onto Center Street and disappeared.

boozed up *adjective* drunk

hippy, **hippie** *noun* a young person who rejects middle-class attitudes toward such things as dress and making money

redneck *noun* a tough, working-class white man from a rural area

mullet-headed *adjective* having a mullet hairstyle (with hair short on top and long on the sides and back)

beatdown *noun* a successful attack, often physical

hairy eyeball *noun* a look that shows disapproval. Usually used with *get, give,* or *shoot.*

take the cake be better, worse, more extreme, etc., than all others

Notice that the blogger adds or substitutes **shit** to make different slang words. **Shithole** has about the same meaning as **hole** (see Unit 44) but is more offensive. **Shitlocks** is an insulting name for *dreadlocks*. A "30.6" is a type of rifle.

The next blogger seems to find everything about life terrible!

My life plainly sucks big time, ya know? It doesn't get better, it just gets worse. And here I thought that it'd be great if nothing goes wrong, but it's all downhill even before this vacation. I'm definitely pissed!

I got back my grades, and they suck! My whole grade point average is horrible. I've gotta take it really slow next time. Just focus on, like, 2 subjects the whole semester. I don't give a shit now. My summer has only just started, and its already the pits. Christ. I really hate my life right now.

I got a call saying that I've flunked my physics paper this morning. WTF? When the hell am I gonna get my degree! ever? It's totally my fault to hand it in 2 days late, I know, and I've flunked 'cause of that. It's horrible, it's really really horrible. I wish I could just get rid of all this crap and start again. But its never gonna happen. I'm always saying, "okay, I'm gonna make it happen this time" but totally blowing it. Nothing gives me any motivation. I really am pissed at myself.

You already know **big time**, **the pits**, **suck**, **blowing it**, **pissed**, and **crap**, as well as **I don't give a shit**. Your "grade point average" is the average of all the grades you've received at school or university, and "all downhill" means "constantly getting worse." Let's hope your life is better than his!

147

Try It!

Think of something that happened recently that really irritated you. Write about it in a paragraph or two. Try to write in slang, using any words you have learned in this book, and write in a way that others will enjoy reading.

It's a Love Thing

One purpose of Internet *groups* (also called *forums* or *newsgroups*) is for people to get and give information and advice. In the message below, from a group where people discuss the problems between men and women, a man asks for advice about his failed relationship. Read his question, then see what people say to him. *Warning:* People express their opinions freely in groups, and some of the language may be offensive!

The question:

I just got dumped by this chick who I started dating a month ago.

She broke up with her ex about 2 months before that because he wouldn't pop the question after 3 years (according to her). I guess he either found out about me, or was struck by lightning coz he promised her he had changed and now they're going out.

I don't think she really knows what she's doing. Most women think I'm a hunk; I checked out her ex once and he's a real nerd. Should I try to get back in tight with her? This is the first girl I really feel like getting hitched to. I even talked about a prenup with her as a way of getting into the subject and she seemed OK with that.

The responses:

from Michelle: IMO the reason anyone leaves anyone else is because one of them changes in some way. In your case, your now-ex gf wised up to the fact that you're a vain jerk who judges people by their looks and is worried that people are after his money.

from Roscoe: you got some good sex out of the skank, move on and look for new fresh meat. She seems pretty flaky, now I see why the divorce rate is so high. Her ex will take her to the curb in a couple of weeks, he just didn't like the fact that his old squeeze was shagging another guy.

from Bernie: She was seeing this guy before you, right? Here's my take on that: chicks are fickle. Leave her completely alone now, and by the time she gets tired of this guy again, you might stand a chance. The chick probably just wants to keep you on a string — it's an ego trip for her having someone waiting.

The responses continued:

from Hilda: You need to find out why she prefers this guy who you think is a loser. If so many women think you're such a good catch, how come you're still single?

from Duane: No bitch worth shit is gonna marry you with a prenup unless you're so freakin loaded that you both know why she's there (rent). Wise up, ditch the bitch and get on with your life.

from Vicki: Duh! Don't you get it? She was only using you to make him jealous — obviously after she'd tried everything else to get him with the program. Lucky for her it worked. Too bad for you though. Now she's probably found the guy that will keep her happy the rest of her life, and you're still paddling around in your own shit.

IMO *abbreviation* in my opinion

gf *abbreviation* girlfriend

hitched *adjective* married

ex *noun* a former boyfriend, girlfriend, husband, or wife

fresh meat *noun* new sexual partners (may be offensive)

good catch *noun* someone who would make a good husband or wife

hunk *noun* a young, attractive, and muscular man

loser /luɪzəˈ/ *noun* a person who is never successful and has few attractive qualities

prenup /priː nʌp/ *noun* prenuptial agreement (a legal agreement that is signed before a marriage and limits how much money or property each person can take if there is a divorce)

skank *noun* a woman who has sex with a lot of men (offensive to women)

take *noun* a personal opinion or interpretation: "He gave us his take on why we lost."

break up *phrasal verb* end a romantic relationship

wise up *phrasal verb* learn some important information

ditch *verb* get rid of someone or something

shag *verb* have sex with someone

get with the program understand what is happening and act appropriately. If you **get sb with the program**, you do what is required to make someone understand a situation.

pop the question ask someone to marry you

Try It!

I. **What's your advice? Read the man's question and the responses to it again. Then write about 50 words of advice that you think would help him, using slang vocabulary.**

_____

_____

_____

_____

_____

_____

_____

II. **Do you have a love problem? We hope not! But everyone has had one at one time or another. Write a paragraph or two, 100-150 words long, describing your problem (past or present) and what advice you need. Then, if you're brave, find a group where people give advice (by going to one of the sites listed at "Let Your Fingers Do the Talkin'") and post your question there.**

_____

_____

_____

_____

_____

_____

_____

_____

_____

_____

_____

_____

_____

_____

_____

Down in Flames

Many Internet groups attract people who have very strong—and often negative—opinions. People whose opinions are unpopular or unacceptable find it easier to express themselves on the Internet, because they don't have to talk face-to-face and can be completely anonymous.

Expressing angry, hostile, or hateful opinions in e-mail or in Internet groups is called **flaming**. It isn't a good idea to participate in **flaming**! However, reading some of the messages that people post can be useful for learning the slang that people use when they're angry. Look at the conversation in this group, in which people exchange insults while they talk about a controversial movie (*The Passion of the Christ*, a religious film directed by Mel Gibson), and their different opinions about the president. Alpha, TallTex, Cleaver, and star_witness are the names that these writers use (obviously not their real names).

Alpha> If you're into two hours of watching a guy gettin the shit whupped outta him, step right up, because that's what The Passion is about.

TallTex> Yeah, that's pretty much what David Edelstein (note the jewish name) calls it in his review: The Jesus Chainsaw Massacre. That's america for you. Nobody is allowed to do anything that displeases the jews.

Cleaver> I say the guy's dead on. Its a snuff movie with more violence than an Italian zombie flick.

Alpha> Get real. It's shit propaganda from religious weirdos. Don't try to give it more meaning than it has. And lay off the Jews, the movie does enough bashing there.

star_witness> Gimme a break!! So The Ten Commandments is out because it coulda made people hate Egyptians? Just because you don't have Christ in your lives, you totally miss the point.

Cleaver> Uh, excuse me! Did I miss the sign on the door that said "bible-thumpers welcome"? Actually, I was bored shitless through most of it.

TallTex> Oh, I get it. Alpha is a yid and star_witness is born-again Bible-belter. Let's get that straight.

Cleaver> I guess that makes you an ignorant slut and a fucking racist asshole. Or did I miss something again?

Alpha> Yeah, the fact that you're a clueless fuckwit. Let's stick to the movie – which, historically speaking, is just a crock anyway. There are more lies in it than the Bush administration deals out in a week.

TallTex> Hello? Weren't we going to talk about the movie here and how the kikes lobbied for Gibson to go soft on the historical hymies?

> Cleaver> It's worth pointing out that Bush, who I agree is a lying sack of shit, hasn't got the brains or the balls to do what Gibson did: put a wad of dough on the line and share the passion of his faith.
>
> Alpha> Some risk. You could put a piece of crap in a theater and label it "Poop, by Mel Gibson" and it would make 25 million.
>
> star_witness> I wouldn't expect shit-for-brains, yellowbelly useless slimeballs like you clowns to understand courage, faith or any human traits worth having. As for Mr. Bush, guess what? He won the election, so deal with it, you low-rent douchebags.

The following terms are all considered strong insults by some group. They're never used in polite speech, and many people would find all of them offensive:

bible-thumper *noun* a Christian who is too enthusiastic about spreading religion

douchebag /duɪʃ bæg/ *noun* an irritating and stupid person

fuckwit *noun* a stupid person

hymie *noun* Jew (very offensive)

kike *noun* Jew (very offensive)

yid *noun* Jew (very offensive)

lying sack of shit *noun* a liar

scumbag, **slimeball** *noun* a disgusting person with no morals

shit-for-brains *noun* an idiot

slut *noun* a woman (now sometimes a man) with no sexual morals

weirdo /wiə-doʊ/ *noun* a strange or weird person

yellowbelly /jɛloʊ bɛli/ *noun* a coward

Other vocabulary:

dead on *adjective* exactly correct

low-rent *adjective* cheap, inferior

shitless *adverb* a lot. **Shitless** is usually used after the adjectives *bored* and *scared*.

balls *noun* courage (literally, a man's testicles). Many people find this word offensive.

snuff movie *noun* a film in which someone is actually killed

lay off *phrasal verb* stop doing something; stop criticizing or bothering someone

be into sb/sth be very interested in someone or something

Deal with it take action to solve a problem

You Decide

60

Let's assume that you have a choice of many different movies to see, but you don't know which ones are good. Your friends can't help—they haven't seen them either! Why not go to an Internet group to see what people are saying about one of the movies that interests you? Nearly all of the Web sites that sell DVDs or movie tickets have a forum where people can write their opinions. Popular movie sites that host groups include www.imdb.com, www.rottentomatoes.com, www.spout.com, www.flixster.com, and www.metacritic.com.

Here are some opinions about a film called *Dawn of the Dead*. *Dawn of the Dead* is about zombies, people who return to life after they have died and do violent and cruel things. This version is a remake, a second version of a film that was first made many years ago.

These folks liked the movie:

I really liked this new version of Dawn of the dead. It wasn't a splatter movie like Braindead which was just crap. And the ending: I woulda never thought that something this radical would happen after credits. This is a winner for everybody who likes zombie films.

--

If you like balls-out gory horror, you'll love this flick. If you don't, you won't. When I heard the original was being remade I was pissed. Every time a horror classic has been remade since 1987 it has sucked. But this new Dawn of the Dead rocks, and it's bloody as hell to boot. This is not a stupid-ass video-game zombie movie. It's got big-time blood and guts all over the place.

--

Whoever gives this film a bad rating is a class A tool. Hard to say which was better, this one or the original. Prolly the original, but this film pretty much stomps all other zombie films.

--

What a kickass movie. there is no better zombie movie out there. Action-packed with lots of blood and gore. KICKASS.

These guys didn't:

Why does this movie suck? Here you go. Let's start by saying it lacked what you need in a survival movie: good characters. If four or five people told the story instead of a dozen plus, the quality woulda shot way up. I only remember one character, Sarah: all the others sorta blended into each other. And another thing: would you go into a zombie-infested place just to save a dog?

--

The zombies themselves are just monsters, the film doesn't even tell you they used to be ordinary people with normal lives. Remember how in the original you kinda felt sorry for the dead sometimes? Remember when that nun zombie gets her skirt thingy stuck in a door and then somebody unlocks the door just to let the nun go? How great is that? Totally. You don't get any of that in the remake.

--

It blows "28 Days Later" out of the water, but that's not saying much. The scariest part of this movie is the ten bucks you spend on it at the ticket booth.

These people liked some things about the film and didn't like others:

This movie sucks worse then anything that has ever sucked before. Then again, the blood and gore rocked.

--

I gave it 8 outta 10 It's not as awesome as the original but it makes up for it with tons of action and tons of gore. Two people get HUGE chunks of skin bitten off them with lots of blood spurting, we see loadsa slimy body parts and even a little gut munching. One thing I didn't like: The director has this weird obsession with slow-motion: he always shows the people's feet in slo-mo, and all this other stuff: somebody flicking a cigarette, then some dude stepping on it, then some chick washing her hands in the water, all of it in slo-mo. What's that about?

--

Maybe I'm a little too oldschool but I loved this movie: it coulda been an over-hyped cheesy imitation, but it's not. It's mainly about blowing up heads and they do it well. Here's some stuff I didn't like. 1) The #1 thing that got on my nerves was too many characters. In the original, there were four characters. In this one, there are fifteen. They're mostly OK, especially Ving Rhames, the badass cop with a ginormous gun, but how the heck are ya sposta remember who's who? 2) When did zombies learn to run? Zombies are dead! That means their limbs stiffen and they lurch around until ya shoot'em in the head! 3) The way the zombie-baby scene played out was kinda stupid, tho the baby itself is freakin' awesome.

balls-out *adjective* complete; total; without any restraint (may be offensive)

kickass *adjective* very good. If something **kicks ass** (may be offensive) or **kicks butt**, it's impressive.

flick *noun* a movie

splatter movie *noun* a movie with a lot of blood and violence

tool *noun* a stupid person

give sth 8 (3, 6, etc.) out of 10 a way of saying how good or bad you think something is, when 10 is a perfect score.

How _____ is that? a way to express an opinion with a question. "How great is that?" means "That's really great."

What's that about? a question that people ask to show that they think there's no good reason for something.

Try It!

Have you seen any movies lately? Why not write a review of one and post it on the Web at one of the movie sites? Use some slang to say what you liked and what you didn't like. Look at Unit 32 again to see some of the things people notice about movies.

_____

_____

_____

_____

_____

_____

_____

_____

_____

_____

_____

_____

_____

61 Cut to the Chase

Even after you have heard and used a lot of slang, the conversations you see in chat rooms may look confusing at first. You might wonder if some of it is even English!

People in chat rooms—like people who send instant messages or who text each other—use a lot of slang and very simple spelling. It's much shorter and faster than writing standard English.

When you **cut to the chase**, you stop talking about unimportant things so that you can focus on what is important. That's how people chat when they have to use their fingers: everything that's difficult or wordy is left out! Instead, you focus on what you can say fast. Chat-room language is just like instant-messaging language, and very similar to texting language.

Look at this conversation in a chat room. The speakers here all seem to know each other in real life.

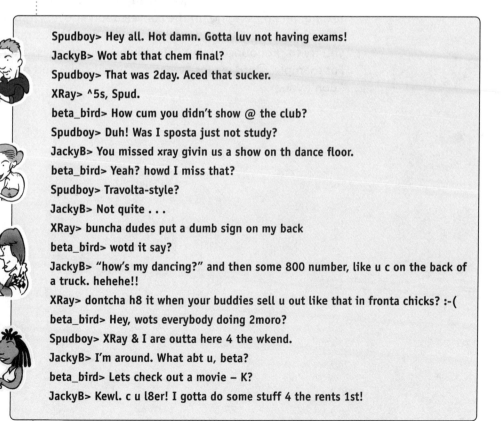

Spudboy> Hey all. Hot damn. Gotta luv not having exams!

JackyB> Wot abt that chem final?

Spudboy> That was 2day. Aced that sucker.

XRay> ^5s, Spud.

beta_bird> How cum you didn't show @ the club?

Spudboy> Duh! Was I sposta just not study?

JackyB> You missed xray givin us a show on th dance floor.

beta_bird> Yeah? howd I miss that?

Spudboy> Travolta-style?

JackyB> Not quite . . .

XRay> buncha dudes put a dumb sign on my back

beta_bird> wotd it say?

JackyB> "how's my dancing?" and then some 800 number, like u c on the back of a truck. hehehe!!

XRay> dontcha h8 it when your buddies sell u out like that in fronta chicks? :-(

beta_bird> Hey, wots everybody doing 2moro?

Spudboy> XRay & I are outta here 4 the wkend.

JackyB> I'm around. What abt u, beta?

beta_bird> Lets check out a movie – K?

JackyB> Kewl. c u l8er! I gotta do some stuff 4 the rents 1st!

Wots Nu?

The language used in chat rooms, instant messages, and text messages is always *short*. To understand it, you may have to think about letters and symbols in a new way. Here are some points to keep in mind:

• The names of letters, rather than their sounds, are often used to make short words even shorter. For example, **c** means "see," and **u** means "you."

• Some numbers, particularly **2**, **4**, and **8**, can take the place of sounds. **2** can stand for "to," "too," and the sound /tu/. **4** can stand for "for" and the sound /foɚ/. **8** often stands for the sound /eɪt/, as in **l8er** ("later"), **h8** ("hate"), and **str8** ("straight").

• Symbols on the keyboard sometimes take the place of words or meanings. You know already that **@** means "at" and **&** means "and." Another useful symbol is **^**, which can mean "up" or "high"; **^5s** means **high fives** (see Unit 45).

• Spelling is very careless in chat rooms. People often type just enough letters so that you can recognize a word. In the conversation above, **abt** means "about," **wot** means "what," **wkend** means "weekend," and **luv** means "love."

• Other shortcuts that you have already learned are common in chat, texting, and messaging. In the conversation above, **chem** stands for "chemistry." A contracted word or phrase may look strange, but if you try to pronounce it you'll usually be able to guess what it means. For example, **wotd** means "what'd" ("what did") and **dontcha** means "don't you."

Try It!

I. Here are some chat-room lines. Translate them into standard English, supplying whatever words are needed to make complete sentences.

1. d'you run some kinda legit biz?

_____

2. Whoz the QT I saw u w/last nite?

_____

3. I thot u were here 1ce b4.

_____

4. Gotta go. CUL8ER.

_____

5. Heckuva pic u sent. Wherd u get the tan?

_____

6. Its EZ. I jus ditched the g/f.

_____

II. Now see if you can translate these sentences into chat-room language. Make them as short as you can while still being clear!

1. You're too late; why didn't you call me at home this morning?

_____

2. Wait—before you mosey, can anyone come in for you tonight?

_____

3. Just because people are new doesn't mean you have to disrespect them.

_____

62 TXT U L8R

From your study of English, you know the word *text* as a noun. But today *text* is also often used as a verb, meaning "send someone a cell-phone text message."

Many cell phones have only a numeric keypad, which makes it difficult to spell out words, and text messages are supposed to be short—no more than 160 characters long. So texters (people who send text messages) have every reason to cut to the chase.

A person sending an instant message (IM) is usually sitting at a full computer keyboard, but IMers (people who send IMs) like to keep their messages short as well, so they use some of the same shortcuts that they use when texting.

Here's a "conversation" between two friends who are leaving messages for each other on their cell phones. See if you can figure out what's going on.

> Monday 7:30pm: RUOK? U DONT ANSER. WOT ABOUT TIX?
>
> Tuesday 1:12am: YO. STUCK @ WRK. WILL GET TIX 2MORO.
>
> Tuesday 10:00am: SOOOO? UR FONE IS BROKE, RITE?
>
> Tuesday 12:07pm: SRY. MEETINGS. @ LNCH NOW, GOT TIX. WHER R U?
>
> Tuesday 2:30pm: :-)) NEED 2 TLK. WHEN?
>
> Tuesday 3:35pm: IM ME F U C ME ONLINE AFTR 4

Later they continue their "conversation" by messaging when they're both online.

ROSCOE: **Bin waitin' for ya, girl. You jes get home?**

MICHELLE: **I'm at the library. Internet packed up @ home. Can we talk on the phone now?**

ROSCOE: **No can do girl; gotta look like I'm workin.**

MICHELLE: **Here's the deal: my cousins in town. Can U get her a ticket?**

ROSCOE: **You mean . . . whats-her-name. The one from Memphis.**

MICHELLE: **Yeah, Natalie.**

ROSCOE: **They didn't have 3 seats together. I got us 1 of the last pairs.**

MICHELLE: **R U jes sayin that coz you hate her?**

ROSCOE: **No way! That's 4 real.**

MICHELLE: **Hows bout Natalie 'n me sittin together, and you in a single nearby?**

ROSCOE: **:-(**

MICHELLE: **OK, you sit w/her and I'll sit alone**

ROSCOE: **:'-(Y R U bustin my balls girl?**

MICHELLE: **Yer such a QT when yer mad! We'll meet you there. THX. IOU1.**

Texting and messaging are easy to understand if you think about how the characters sound. But there are even more shortcuts than the ones you see in chat rooms. Here are some of the most common ones:

R	are
8	ate
B	be
4	for
F	if
C	see
2	to or too
Y	why
U	you

These characters and others are often combined to make longer words:

B4	before
QT	cutie
D8	date
EZ	easy
L8R	later
NE1	anyone

There are also many common short versions of words that are used in texting and messaging, such as **THX** for "thanks," **BTW** for "by the way," **LOL** for "laughing out loud," and so forth. To find lists of these on the Web, search for "SMS Dictionary."

pack up *phrasal verb* stop working

bust sb's balls cause problems for someone, usually a man (may be offensive)

no can do I can't do that

GET THE PICTURE?

In instant messages, e-mail, and sometimes text messages, people use punctuation marks to make pictures that stand for words. These pictures are called *emoticons* (a combination of *emotion* and *icon*). You have to use your imagination to understand what they mean. The most common emoticon is the happy face :-) (you have to look at it sideways). A sad face looks like :-(. The emoticon ;-) shows that you are making a joke (because one eye is winking). To find the most common emoticons, search on the Web for "emoticons." After learning a few, you can use your imagination to make new ones.

Try It!

I. Write the standard or slang English word for each of the following shorthand words used in texting and messaging. Some of them are used in this unit; for the others, you will have to think about what the letters sound like.

1. TLK _____

2. THX _____

3. RUOK _____

4. BCNU _____

5. TIX _____

6. PIX _____

7. CU L8R _____

II. Write a texting version of each of the following sentences. Some of these are found in this unit; for others, you can use whatever you think will work. Hint: Texters often leave out vowels but keep consonants when they shorten words.

1. I owe you one. _____

2. I'm at work. _____

3. Are you for real? _____

4. It's easier at night. _____

5. Don't be any later than 5. _____

ANSWER KEY

The answers to all the exercises in this book are given here. For many exercises, there is more than one possible answer. When there are only two or three possible answers, all of them are given here. However, if the answers can vary a great deal, what you will find here is a *possible* correct answer. If you have doubts about any of your answers, ask your teacher or a qualified native speaker.

UNIT A: Yo!

Your answers may vary. Here are some possible answers.

1. Dude! What's up?
2. Nada. How about you?
3. Hey girl. What's shakin?
4. Yo! Whatcha been up to?

UNIT B: Gimme a Break!

1. What is shaking? (No one would ever say it like this!)
2. How are you getting home?
3. Where did you go last night?
4. Why is it taking so long?
5. Why has it taken so long?

UNIT C: Say What?

1. Is anybody sitting here?
2. What have you got in the box?
3. How long have you been waiting here?
4. Do you know that guy over there?
5. Why is she driving your car?

UNIT D: Word!

I

1. **zip** means "zero" or "nothing."
2. **bananas** in this sentence means "crazy."
3. **mega** means "very big"
4. **total** in this sentence means "completely wreck."
5. **huffy** means "impatient and annoyed."
6. **pothead** means "someone who smokes marijuana a lot."

II

1. D 4. C
2. B 5. A
3. F 6. E

UNIT 1: Who You Talkin' To?

I

1. **How** ya doin' with the new job? **How are** you doing with the new job?
2. **Who** ya rootin' for in the game? **Who are** you rooting for in the game?
3. **Whatcha** doin' this weekend? **What are you** doing this weekend?
4. **Where** ya been the last two hours? **Where have** you been the last two hours?
5. **When** ya comin' back from Dallas? **When are you** coming back from Dallas?
6. **Who** ya votin' for? **Who are** you voting for?
7. **Whatcha** got planned for Friday? **What have you** got planned for Friday?

II

1. **Do you** need a lift?
2. **Have you** got any ideas? *or* Do you have any ideas?
3. **Do you** mind if I borrow your watch?
4. **Do you** want to see what I bought?
5. **Have you** seen any good movies lately?
6. **Are you** finished with that? *or* **Have you** finished with that?

UNIT 2: Chow Time

I

I don't think I'm that much of a **chowhound**, but after I finish working out I can really **shovel it in**. My favorite thing to **pig out** on is macaroni and cheese: it's not the most healthy **grub**, but it cooks fast. I can usually **down** a whole box of it. My mom tells me I shouldn't **wolf down** my food, but when you're hungry and in a hurry, that's what you gotta do!

II

(Answers will vary.)

UNIT 3: Hot or Cool?

1. Bummer!	4. Bingo!
2. Sweet!	5. Duh!
3. Whatever!	6. Uh-oh!

UNIT 4: Too Cool for School

I

1. You **oughta** have your head examined!	**ought to**
2. **Didja** see the look on his face?	**did you**
3. We're **sposta** stay here till they get back.	**supposed to**
4. I think you're headed for a **lotta** trouble.	**lot of**
5. I **dunno** why he never called me back.	**don't know**
6. Isn't that **kinda** like cheating?	**kind of**
7. **C'mon**, I haven't got all day.	**come on**
8. Don't you **hafta** take the test again?	**have to**
9. I **betcha** we get back before they do.	**bet you**

II

1. Could you wait here a minute?
2. You let your girlfriend use your credit card?
3. Set your stuff down and relax a while.
4. What would your mother do if she caught you?
5. She said you're a lazy bum.
6. Have you got your passport yet?
7. How often should you change the filter?
8. Have your had your last exam yet?
9. It'll bite you if you hold your hand out.

UNIT 5: Know Your Critters

1. That was the quarterback's problem and not the fault of the **zebra**.
2. The whole country has gone **cuckoo** for low-carb diets.
3. She's a **snake** and she'll betray you the minute you turn your back.
4. If he loses this time, you can consider him a dead **duck**.
5. They were going to flip over a parked police car, but I **chickened** out and went home.
6. It's a great house, but it's a **bear** to keep clean.
7. I tried to run down the escalator but there was this **cow** in front of me and I couldn't get around her.
8. It's the worst detective novel I have ever read—a real **turkey**.
9. They lost the first game in overtime and then got **skunked** in the second one, 20-2.
10. The insurance company is trying to **weasel** out of paying claims from the flood damage.
11. His last girlfriend was an actress and she was a real **fox**, but the one he's got now is a **dog**.
12. Lots of the big **fish** have bought land on the island and put up huge houses.

UNIT 6: How Much Ya Talkin' About?

I

These are possible answers; your own answers will vary.

1. I thought the mayor's speech was a load of nonsense.
2. They showed us a slew of photos from their vacation.
3. You're gonna be in heaps of trouble if you don't clean this up.
4. She made gobs of money in real estate and retired young.
5. I cooked a ton of food and then no one came.
6. We had loads of time so we went to a movie.
7. Nothing ever satisfies that bunch of crybabies.
8. Tons of paper got thrown away because it was all printed wrong.

II

1. Like where?
2. Like when?
3. Like how many?
4. Like what?
5. Like how?
6. Like which ones? *or* Like who?

UNIT 7: Words Fail Me

I

1. information
2. snow
3. ingredients
4. furniture

II

1. I **kinda** like rock music, I just don't like doing it myself, **you know**? **I mean** I love the Stones. One of my favorite singers is Bruce Springsteen. But, who else? I dunno. There's a lot of **stuff**. The Sex Pistols I **sorta** like — **guys** like that. **The thing is**, I don't know that much from earlier. **I mean** I really don't know any of the dead artists. Except I know Fats Waller and he's amazing. Most of the stuff I listen to now is **like** ambient or instrumental. **I guess** I should probably get to know more of those early guys—Frank Sinatra and Dean Martin and **guys** like that. There's **loads of shit** I've only heard once or twice that I should probably **kinda** study **or something**.

2. I like rock music, I just don't like doing it myself. I love the Stones. One of my favorite singers is Bruce Springsteen. But, who else? I dunno. There's a lot of music I like. The Sex Pistols I like — bands like that. I don't know that much from earlier. I really don't know any of the dead artists. Except I know Fats Waller and he's amazing. Most of the music I listen to now is ambient or instrumental. I should probably get to know more of those early singers—Frank Sinatra and Dean Martin and singers like that. There's a lot of music I've only heard once or twice that I should study.

UNIT 8: Ka-Ching!

The following are possible answers. You may have thought of others that are also correct.

1. four tens and two fives; 50 bucks/smackers/clams (etc.); four sawbucks and a couple of five-spots
2. a wad of cash; loads of dead presidents; folding money
3. eight bucks and some change; a five and three singles; less than ten bucks

UNIT 9: Low on Dough?

I

HEATHER: Tiff? Hot news. Jason just gave Whitney an engagement ring.
TIFFANY: You're kidding! Wasn't he supposed to be totally **broke/busted**?
HEATHER: Well I guess not. The thing **set** him **back** 3,000 bucks.
TIFFANY: Jason **blew/dropped** three **grand** on an engagement ring?
HEATHER: He must've maxed out three credit cards to do it. And knowing him, he **got taken.** He doesn't have the sense to know what things cost.
TIFFANY: I heard his parents are **loaded/flush** and they'll bail him out if he's in debt.
HEATHER: Well get this: Whitney is already talking about having a wedding reception at the Ritz!
TIFFANY: Either her parents are crazy or they have very **deep pockets**.

II

The following answers are examples; your sentences will vary.

1. I could tell that she was a gold digger when she asked me how much I made.
2. Fifty bucks is chump change compared to what they charge you for parking illegally.
3. If I had a wad of cash the first thing I'd do is spend a week on the beach.
4. How could he say he was broke and then blow a hundred bucks on a bottle of tequila?
5. I'll betcha 50 smackers that I get back before you do.
6. The last time I ordered CDs from them I really got taken to the cleaners.
7. Is that supposed to be a designer hairstyle? Wow! How much did they take you for?

UNIT 10: Check This Out

1. Somebody goofed them up and we have to start over again.
2. You're really going to tick him off if you break that off.
3. If you don't wolf it down we're going to be late.
4. They kicked her out because she was never on time.
5. They ripped them off at a flea market.
6. I can't believe you were stupid enough to flip him off!
7. Why don't you get together with her and work it out?
8. He said he picked her up at a mall.

UNIT 11: If Ya Can't Beat 'em, Join 'em

The exercise sentences are shown here, with pronunciations given for the underlined words.

1. How /dɪdʒə/ find /əm/ so fast?
2. I /ˈtoʊldʒə/ guys we should've dropped /əm/ off first.
3. She asked /əm/ if /idˈgɑːtʃə/ a present.
4. Why /ˈdoʊntʃə/ try to pick /ɚ/ up?
5. /ˈdɪdʒɑːl/ hear what /ət/ costs to bring /əm/ back?
6. They're not gonna /ˈlɛtʃə/ keep /əm/.
7. /jə/ should've checked /əm/ out before you bought /əm/.
8. I know /ɪtlˈsɛtʃə/ back at least a grand.
9. I /ˈsɛdʒə/ guys couldn't stay long enough to bail /ɚ/ out.

UNIT 12: Sack Time

I

These sentences are examples of correct answers; your sentences will differ.

1. Sometimes I like to rack out in the back of my car.
2. I need at least seven hours of sack time at night.
3. I take a short snooze if I need to in the late afternoon.
4. Friday and Saturday night I usually don't crash till after midnight.
5. The best time to catch some Z's is right after lunch.
6. After a day with lots of meetings I'm always totally wiped out.
7. Usually I like to try to get a little extra shut-eye on weekends.

II

1. Let's go down to the beach and catch some pix.
2. We had to leave early and only caught a few tracks.
3. They went to New York to catch some plays.
4. We stayed home last night and caught some vids.

UNIT 13: You Shoulda Been There!

1. Of course you **gotta/hafta** pay it all. I **coulda/shoulda/musta** told you that.
2. You **coulda/mighta/woulda** gotten the job if you'd dressed for the interview.
3. Who **woulda/coulda** guessed that they were married all this time?
4. It **woulda** been nice if you'd warned me they were coming.
5. I can't go, I really **gotta/hafta** study tonight.
6. She **shoulda/coulda** got rid of all that stuff; now she's **gotta** store it.

UNIT 14: All Tooled Up

1. We really got **screwed** on the tickets because we bought them at the last minute.
2. Why should I **fork over** a hundred bucks when there's no guarantee I'll get the room?
3. **Pump** him for all the latest gossip from the dorm.
4. Because of the budget cuts, they had to **ax** ten jobs.
5. The newspapers continued to **hammer away** at the governor.
6. Why don't we **hook up** sometime next week and talk about it?

UNIT 15: Ain't No Point

1. It's none of your business *or* It isn't any of your business.
2. I'm not going anywhere.
3. There isn't anyone smarter than him *or* No one is smarter than him.
4. He hasn't ever worked a day in his life.
5. She's no fashion model *or* She isn't a fashion model.

6. I'm not going to let you get away with it.
7. They're not wearing any clothes.
8. It's not what you think it is.

UNIT 16: A Clip Joint

1. How **'bout** going to the beach this weekend? **about**
2. After he got arrested, his **cred** went way up with the drug dealers. **credibility**
3. There wasn't anybody there **'cept** three jocks. **except**
4. Her uncle's an old **lech** who's always trying to paw my leg. **lecher**
5. Who's your **rep** in Congress? **representative**
6. Email me a **pic** so I'll recognize you when we meet. **picture**
7. Check and see if there's any **veggies** in the **fridge**. **vegetables, refrigerator**

UNIT 17: Yer Yankin' My Chain   (No exercises)

UNIT 18: Got Wheels?

A1 – B8	A6 – B5
A2 – B3	A7 – B9
A3 – B2	A8 – B1
A4 – B4	A9 – B6
A5 – B7	

UNIT 19: Howdja Do?

The underlined parts of the sentences are shown here in pronunciation symbols and the sentences are written out in standard English below.

1. /ˈwaɪdʒəˈlɛtʃɚ/ hair get so long?
   Why did you let your hair get so long?
2. I didn't think you'd wanna talk /tuwɚ/.
   I didn't think you would want to talk to her.
3. /ˈwaɪdʒəˈgɪmi/ only five bucks?
   Why did you give me only five bucks?
4. /ˈhuːdʒə/ say /ˈgɑːtʃɚ/ tickets?
   Who did you say got your tickets?
5. I /ˈniːdʒə/ to do lotsa stuff.
   I need you to do lots of things.
6. /ˈhaʊdʒəˈsiːjəm/ from that far away?
   How did you see them from that far away?
7. He'd help if you'd just /ˈgɪvəm/ a chance.
   He would help if you would just give him a chance.
8. We'd have stayed if we'd /ˈgɑːtʃɚ/ message.
   We would have stayed if we had gotten your message.
9. /ˈhaʊdʒə/ know he was gonna bomb?
   How did you know he was going to bomb?
10. /ˌweɚdʒəˈgɛtʃɚ/ new laptop?
    Where did you get your new laptop?

UNIT 20: When Ya Gotta Go . . .   (No exercises)

UNIT 21: Nail That Sucker!

1. E   2. C   3. D   4. B   5. F   6. A

UNIT 22: **The Grim Reaper**

I

Here are examples of correct sentences. Your sentences may be slightly different.

1. My computer's out of whack.
2. Maybe he's got the runs.
3. No, I think I'm gonna hurl.
4. Nah, he popped his clogs about a year ago.
5. The smell in there was about to make me puke.
6. She passed out and they took her to the hospital.
7. It's not working; the battery's kaput.
8. The old one bought the farm.

II

Here is the passage with only the correct expressions:

When I came into Grandpa's room he was puking on his tray. I tried to call the nurse but the phone was out of whack. I hoofed it out into the hallway to find someone. A doctor finally came, but by then it was too late: the old man had already bought the farm.

UNIT 23: **Scope This**

These sentences are possible answers; yours should be very similar.

1. Don't cave just 'cause the kids are screaming.
2. The team is bummed 'cause they got totally whopped.
3. Where'd ya hang while you were there?
4. She's totally pumped about the wad of cash she made.
5. When I want to chill I go to my 'rents' house in the burbs.
6. Why don't you scope the restaurant to see if it's any good?
7. You should have bailed when he wigged/flipped/freaked.
8. He flipped/freaked/wigged when he saw how much chow they were scarfing up.

UNIT 24: **Uh . . .**

For some of these sentences, there is more than one correct answer.

1. They're **kinda/sorta** dull green and have **lotsa/loadsa** bumps. **kind of/sort of, lots of/loads of**
2. He started acting **kinda/sorta** weird and then ran **outta** the room. **kind of/sort of, out of**
3. Mike Tyson at his peak **coulda** beat anyone!!! **could have**
4. I don't think Kevin Costner **woulda** worked in the Ed Harris role. **would have**
5. Do you **hafta** play that thing so loud or am I **sposta** wear ear plugs? **have to, supposed to**
6. You **musta/shoulda** known they would go in if the door was open. **must have/ should have**
7. It was **kinda/sorta** cool, we learned **lotsa/loadsa** good stuff. **kind of/sort of, lots of/loads of**
8. We're **outta** the clam chowder. You **wanna** try something else? **out of, want to**
9. Don't you think you **oughta** go a little slower? **ought to**
10. You **shoulda/musta** seen the look on her face. **should have/must have**
11. He gave me a **lotta** books to read. **lot of**
12. We're **sposta** meet them here but they **mighta** changed their minds. **supposed to, might have**
13. There's no one home; they **musta** left earlier. I wish I **coulda** talked to them before they left. **must have, could have**
14. They started offering me **loadsa/lotsa** money; what else was I **sposta** do except take it? **loads of/lots of, supposed to**
15. If you **wanna** win, you **hafta/gotta** play the game. **want to, have to/(have) got to**

UNIT 25: Great Bod!

I

1. fists
2. mouth
3. eyes
4. feet
5. hands
6. nose
7. teeth
8. face or mouth
9. hands

II

1. When he smiles, you can see he's got a few **ivories** missing.
2. He's a chowhound with a huge **gut** and he doesn't exercise.
3. They've got her on so many meds that she's out of her **gourd** most of the time.
4. Stop sniffling and just wipe your **schnoz**.
5. He dipped one **tootsy** in the water and said it was too cold.
6. She wears a ring on her **pinkie** with a huge diamond in it.
7. I keep getting e-mails that tell me I can have bigger **boobs**.
8. I looked him right in his **baby blues** and said "No way."
9. She's not too steady on her **pins** since the hip replacement.

UNIT 26: By the Numbers

These sentences are examples only; your sentences will be different.

I think a couple of C-notes will take care of the problem.
We spent 20 bucks on lottery tickets and didn't win diddly.
She takes half a dozen meds and still pukes all the time.
He'll have a gazillion excuses for why he's late.
I've been there half a dozen times but never seen the museum.
He picks up clunkers for nada and then repairs them.
We're not paying him squat till he does the work.
There are umpteen doodads you have to push to make it work.
After their umpteenth visit this year, we told them to stay in a hotel next time.
I understand zilch of what you just said.

UNIT 27: What the Heck Is That?

1. I studied like the devil but I still flunked the test.
2. I'll be darned if I didn't just delete three folders on my hard drive.
3. The police came and scared the crap out of us.
4. Christina Aguilera beats the heck out of Britney Spears any day.
5. Heck if I know.
6. What the dickens took you so long?
7. Boston pounded the heck out of Chicago in last night's game.
8. Didn't she used to go out with Hugo? – Beats the crap out of me.

UNIT 28: To a T

1. What d<u>o</u> <u>you</u> want, a med<u>a</u>l?
2. Wha<u>t</u> <u>a</u>bout a movie, then a li<u>tt</u>le walk?
3. You should <u>have</u> done be<u>tt</u>er than that.
4. I could <u>have</u> told <u>you</u> what <u>a</u> mistake that was.
5. Did <u>you</u> give th<u>e</u>m what they want<u>e</u>d?
6. I heard <u>you</u> might <u>have</u> been trying t<u>o</u> call me.
7. Why did <u>you</u> say she was going t<u>o</u> mee<u>t</u> him?
8. Those have t<u>o</u> be the ho<u>tt</u>est babes <u>a</u>round.
9. What d<u>o</u> <u>you</u> say we ge<u>t</u> <u>a</u> bite t<u>o</u> eat here?

UNIT 29: A Lowlife Gets Nabbed

I

1. She **did time** on a money-laundering **beef**.
2. He **turned rat** in order to **beat the rap on a coke beef**.
3. The **cops nabbed** him for taking a 500-**buck** bribe from a **Fed**.
4. Why would I want to **get in tight** with a **jewelry fence**?
5. They **scammed me** into giving them 200 **clams**.

II

These sentences are examples only; your sentences may be different.

1. He was a drug kingpin with a long rap sheet.
2. She said the cops screwed her over the last time she was nabbed.
3. They'd nailed him in a sting, but he beat the rap.
4. She ran a scam that made wads of cash on overpriced condos.
5. Some lowlife who was trying to avoid doing time on a robbery beef.

UNIT 30: Get Yer Stuff 'n' Go

Here are the sentences in standard English. If you are unsure of the slang pronunciations, ask a native speaker. Remember, when *y* follows *t,* the resulting sound is usually /ʧ/.

1. What a bunch of suckers you all are!
2. You're going to have to let me take them.
3. When have we got to return our stuff and be out of here?
4. What do you say we give him loads of trouble?
5. I'll bet you ten bucks he got your spot.
6. You should have dropped your classes and got yourself a better job.
7. That would have set you back big-time!
8. Did you think I might have forgotten and left you here?
9. Why did you say they are out of tickets?
10. Put your money where your mouth is.

UNIT 31: Knowledge of College

Statement no. 4 is true; all the others are false.

UNIT 32: Whaddaya Think?

I

The sentences shown are not the only possible answers.

1. Except for the lousy sound system, the party really rocked.
2. Two of the singers were sick so the concert was a real turkey.
3. The food at the reception was da bomb, and that kinda made up for the boring speeches.
4. All of the reviews trashed the acting, but I didn't think the movie was that bad.
5. Our hotel room was a little noisy, but the view from the window was awesome!
6. She's got a hot body, but you don't notice it because of the cheesy clothes she wears.
7. She told a totally lame joke and nobody laughed but her.

II

(Answers will vary.)

UNIT 33: Friggin' Intense

1. Isn't it **a little** early to start your **friggin'** moaning?
2. It was so **damn** cold that the **freakin'** pipes froze.

3. That's a **frickin'** lame excuse.
4. Life's too **freakin'** short to put up with such nonsense.
5. This may be **way** stupid, but what did he actually mean?
6. The food was **totally** disappointing, but the show was **kinda** cool.

UNIT 34: **Alien Objects Approaching**

I

1. No one has the **cojones** to tell them they screwed up.
2. If all you're going to do is **kvetch**, why don't you just leave?
3. It's got a flashy video, but the song itself is just **dreck/schlock**.
4. You're gonna be in **beaucoup/mucho** trouble when your dad sees this.
5. He always dates blonde **bimbos** and then wonders why he's bored.
6. We met up with **moi** cousin and had a beer.
7. I'd like to go but I haven't got the **dineros** just now.
8. We just got a **primo** scanner that makes perfect copies.
9. Don't look now, but some **schmuck** just took your parking place.
10. Tina scored **beaucoup** points for handing her paper in early.

II

1. **honcho** *Japanese* big shot; important person; boss
2. **cop** *Dutch* catch; capture; steal
3. **nyet** *Russian* no

UNIT 35: **What's the Buzz?**

These sentences are good examples; your sentences should be similar.

1. They picked up some other guy who took the rap.
2. She had a hotshot lawyer and they knew she'd beat the rap.
3. Everybody is trying to get the lowdown on that.
4. I bet Jake's got the skinny on it.
5. Haven't you heard the buzz? They think *you* did it.
6. Karen and I were dishin' the dirt yesterday.
7. Your sister blabbed it.
8. I was just shootin' the breeze with the homies and it came up.
9. One of his employees gave him a bad rap.
10. He got a bum rap for the way the last deal turned out.

UNIT 36: **Cheap Substitutes**

1. She can **knock back** three martinis and still act normal.
2. I'm going to **throw out** a few ideas to get the conversation started.
3. I think somebody has **made off** with my pen.
4. He's **kissing up** to the boss 'cause he wants Friday off.
5. In that outfit the guys will start **hitting on** you as soon as you walk in.
6. He **kissed off** all of his old clients and now he wants them back.
7. He **knocked** her **up** and now he wants her to get an abortion.
8. When she got hip to the fact that she might get canned, she decided it would be easier to **sell** us all **out**.
9. He's working on a Ph.D. at Princeton, but he always tries to **play** that **down**.

UNIT 37: **Is It Love?**

(Answers will vary according to your experience.)

UNIT 38: If the Shoe Fits . . .

I

These sentences show only one possible solution; your answers will vary.

1. I get a little **spacey** sometimes and forget to check the time, but my boyfriend is a total **flake**.
2. Our **sleazy** mayor got caught taking bribes. He's such a **dirtball**.
3. Which **clueless nitwit** thought that you could drive the car without brakes?
4. He interrupts anyone who's speaking and says something rude—he's just a total **jerk**.

II

These sentences show only one possible solution; your answers will vary.

1. A. Lately she's been really huffy.
   B. I know. What a bitch!
2. A. He's uncool when it comes to clothes.
   B. He's kind of a nerd.
3. A. Did someone say "buff"?
   B. Talk about a stud!
4. A. Unbelievable! She's so ditzy!
   B. Is she a basket case or what?
5. A. I always thought she was hot.
   B. Told you she was a babe.
6. A. How flaky can you get?
   B. She's a major space cadet.

UNIT 39: A Setup Job

I

Your answers should be similar to these.

1. They faked us out, making us think we'd lost electricity.
2. Their agent has asked for a 10% kickback.
3. This is the third government bailout for this company.
4. Somebody's been raking off a huge amount from the casino's profits.
5. Doug's a corporate lawyer, a total sellout.
6. He's really cute, but his bad breath really turns me off.

II

These are possible answers; yours should be somewhat similar.

1. A class in which you can pass even if you blow off most of the homework.
2. When he or she has burned out from working too hard.
3. A huge meal at which everyone pigs out of the food.
4. A movie with lots of blood, killing, and guts that grosses you out.

UNIT 40: It Feels Nice to Say It Twice

I

1 – A	6 – E
2 – C	7 – F
3 – D	8 – H
4 – B	9 – J
5 – I	10 – G

II

1. This lawyer thinks he's a real **hotshot**, but the judge wasn't very impressed.
2. I've been driving in **slo-mo** for the last two hours because of a **fender bender** on the freeway.
3. This theater's only showing a **chick flick** and a **creature feature.**
4. She was totally ticked off with me yesterday, but now she's done a **flip-flop** and

she's all **lovey-dovey.**

5. The best seats in the front are reserved for some **fat cats**, but if there are any **no-shows** you can have their seats.
6. She's got this **itsy-bitsy boob tube** in her kitchen—the screen is only six inches wide.

UNIT 41: Don't Try This at Home

Here are some examples of possible answers; yours will be different.

1. Geez! You'd think they'd be more considerate.
2. Sweet! Maybe I'll take you out to dinner with it.
3. Bummer! Now I'm gonna hafta beat the crap out of you!
4. Holy moly! Don't tell me you were late picking up Gina again.
5. Because the darned thing is already so loud that I have to shout at you!
6. Duh! How long do you want to go without your driver's license?

UNIT 42: Time for Some Answers

Here are some possible answers; yours should be similar.

1. You gonna stop for gas pretty soon?
   a. No way! I've got half a tank.
   b. Yeah, at the next exit.
   c. Criminy, don't tell me you have to pee again.
2. They just said your name over the intercom.
   a. Wow! Are you sure?
   b. Damn, just when I thought I could get out of here.
   c. Cool! They must have found me a seat.
3. Looks like somebody drove into the back of your car.
   a. Damn! Just when I got it back from the garage.
   b. Jeez! Can't I even leave it parked for ten minutes?
   c. Bummer! There go my insurance rates!
4. Did you pass the English test?
   a. Yuppers! Aced that sucker.
   b. Not a chance. That puppy was *hard.*
   c. Who wants to know?

UNIT 43: Win Some, Lose Some

Your sentences will be different from these.

1. Jeanne is the latest hurricane to maul South Florida.
   Florida just got bashed by yet another hurricane.
2. In this state, Republicans got slaughtered at the polls.
   The latest results show the Democrats whupping the Republicans.
3. Senator Laforge hammered the press in his speech.
   The press got slammed by Senator Laforge in a speech.
4. The stock market got clobbered today by rising oil prices.
   Rising oil prices have pounded the stock market.
5. The citrus-fruit crop got walloped by frost.
   Frost has really stomped the citrus-fruit crop.

UNIT 44: What Kinda Place Is This?

I

Your sentences will be different from these.

1. We got stuck in traffic out in the boonies.
2. How'd you like it? I heard it was a dive.

3. She was until she found some dude to shack up with.
4. Nah, I'm outta here—I'm already 20 minutes late.
5. No way! I'm totally not ready to go there.

II

1 – E	7 – G
2 – J	8 – F
3 – A	9 – D
4 – C	10 – K
5 – I	11 – B
6 – H	

UNIT 45: Gimme Some Skin

I

Your answers will be different from these.

1. They were trying to catch a streaker who ran by.
2. Some jerk body-slammed me dancing last night.
3. My belly button is an innie.
4. Looks like she's picked up some sweet arm candy.

II

1 – C	5 – F
2 – A	6 – H
3 – G	7 – E
4 – D	8 – B

UNIT 46: High Life

Some words you chose to replace the underlined words may be different from these.

There was a party last night at Marc's **crib**. There were **loads of** people there and I didn't know anybody. **Some dude** offered me a **joint** but I said **no way**. In one corner some **chicks** were **knocking back** shots of tequila and laughing. I walked toward them and then **some jerk** grabbed my **butt** and said "Hey! Don't I know you?" **I said, "Sorry, sucker,"** and that he should keep his **paws** to himself. I was not liking this party. The music was **way** loud and there was nowhere to **chill**. I decided to **book** and just as I got to the door **a buncha dudes** walked in with guns. I think they were **dopeheads**. They said "Don't nobody move." This **scared the crap out of me**. It got **totally** quiet and then we heard someone in the kitchen on their cell phone — to the **cops**. Next thing, **some smashed bitch** started screaming and one of the **dopers** told her to **shut up**. She **chilled instantly**. Then we heard sirens and two **cop** cars pulled up. The robbers ran through the house, looking for a way out. Then the **cops** caught two of the **dopers** inside, but they also **nailed another guy** who was just at the party: they recognized him **cuz** apparently he was a **doper** who had been running **a coke scam**. Next time Marc invites me to a party I'm **gonna say forget it**!

UNIT 47: Like I Care

I

1. Don't you think the tickets are a little pricey? Who **cares**? Matt said he'd pay.
2. But it's really cold outside. I don't **care** if it's 50 below zero—get out there and shovel the sidewalk!
3. I can't believe it! That puppy peed in every room of the house! What, **like** it's supposed to know better?

II

Your answers will be different from these.

1. **Man, I feel so tired this morning!** Like you didn't spend the whole weekend sleeping!

2. **Bill and Charlotte are really ticked off at you.** So who cares if they don't talk to me.
3. **Isn't this the third time this week she's bailed on us?** She doesn't give a damn about her job.

UNIT 48: In Deep Doo-Doo

Here's what's really got me **down**. Last week when I was cruisin' in the burbs, some lowlife dirtball plowed into me at a red light. The sucker didn't have any insurance! Boy, was I ticked **off**! Now somehow I've gotta pop **for** the repairs myself. I'm totally broke. I tried to hit **up** my girlfriend but she's all tapped **out**. Everybody else just bags **on** me. This will set me **back** 500 bucks! How am I gonna cough **up** that amount?

UNIT 49: Tough Nuts to Crack

The words you choose may be different.

1. That's a <u>bad</u> suit, bro! How much you pay for it? **attractive**
2. I bought these <u>funky</u> '70s disco records last week. **cool**
3. Oh, I get it. You're in such a <u>funky</u> mood today. **irritable**
4. Who knew her singing would be so incredibly <u>bad</u>? **terrible**
5. How come you got the new toaster and I got this <u>funky</u> one? **junky**
6. Come check out this CD—it's got some <u>bad</u> tracks on it. **enjoyable**

UNIT 50: See Ya

(No exercises)

UNIT 51: Word for Word

(No exercises)

UNIT 52: How Some Folks Talk

1. I **have** to remember this place.
2. You need nigga repellent **to** keep them off your ass.
3. You **are** a fine lookin' woman, Jackie.
4. How the fuck **do** they know that?
5. That doesn't mean you **have got** to confirm it.

UNIT 53: They're Playin' Yer Song!

(No exercises)

UNIT 54: Blog Style

With all of this in mind, I could be faced with choosing between this job and the Atlanta job. Maybe. I still haven't been offered anything yet. But if I had to choose, I think I've come to the difficult conclusion that I'd go with the Atlanta job. I'd be working closer to my field of study, in a much more relaxed atmosphere (the corporate world is really not for me). And even though the pay is 50 cents less, there's still opportunity for cash bonuses. I wish the benefits were better, though. And I wouldn't have to serve coffee or doughnuts to anybody.

1. The job in Atlanta
2. The job with the real estate firm
3. The Atlanta job

UNIT 55: Trippin'

(The writing in these exercises is based on your own experience.)

UNIT 56: Vibin'

(The writing in these exercises is based on your own experience.)

UNIT 57: Bitchin'

(The writing in these exercises is based on your own experience.)

UNIT 58: It's a Love Thing

(The writing in these exercises is based on your own experience.)

UNIT 59: Down in Flames

(No exercises)

UNIT 60: You Decide

(The writing in these exercises is based on your own experience.)

UNIT 61: Cut to the Chase

I

1. Do you run some kind of legitimate business?
2. Who's the cutie I saw you with last night?
3. I thought you were here once before.
4. I've got to go. See you later.
5. That's a heck of a picture you sent. Where did you get the tan?
6. It's easy. I just ditched the girlfriend.

II

1. UR 2L8; Y didn't U call me @ home this a.m.?
2. W8: B4 U moZ, can NE1 cum in 4 U 2nite?
3. Jus b/c ppl R nu it doesn mean U hafta diss'em.

UNIT 62: TXT U L8R

I

1. talk
2. Thanks
3. Are you okay?
4. Be seeing you.
5. tickets
6. pictures
7. See you later.

II

1. IOU1
2. IM @ WRK
3. RU4 REAL?
4. ITS EZR @NITE
5. DONT B NE L8R THAN 5

INDEX

Orin Hargraves has worked in lexicography and reference publishing since 1991, making substantial contributions to dictionaries and other reference works from American, British, and European publishers including Bloomsbury, Cambridge University Press, Chambers-Harrap, Facts on File, HarperCollins, Langenscheidt, Longman, Macmillan, Merriam-Webster, and Oxford University Press. Prior to this he had a wide-ranging career as an ESL and EFL teacher, working with Chinese immigrants in the US, lycée students in Morocco, and refugees in London. He is the author of *Mighty Fine Words and Smashing Expressions,* a guide to the differences between British and American English, and he has also written travel guides including *Culture Shock! Morocco* and *London At Your Door*. He lives in Carroll County, Maryland